BOOM OR BUSTED

FAMILY
DOLLARS and SENSE

By Ed Hutka

Logos International
Plainfield, New Jersey

All Scripture references,
unless otherwise noted,
are taken from the King James Version.

BOOM OR BUSTED
Library of Congress Catalog Card Number: 78-71961
International Standard Book Number: 0-88270-337-4
Logos International, Plainfield, New Jersey 07060

Contents

Introduction

WHY I WROTE THIS BOOK

Money really does matter to Christians.

Christians are unnecessarily being ripped off by Satan's system.

It is estimated that over 80 percent of Christian homes have serious financial problems.

More than 50 percent of all divorces can be traced directly to money mismanagement.

Churches do not generally offer a detailed course in "sane money management."

There are more than 1,000 Scriptures relating to personal possessions.

Christ was concerned about money and personal possessions, for He referred to them in sixteen of the thirty-eight parables. "Ye shall know the truth, and the truth shall make you free" (John 8:32).

The story needs to be told. When anyone begins to apply God's simple principles he will begin on a journey towards financial freedom. "Thou hast been faithful over a few things, I will make thee ruler over many things" (Matt. 25:23).

Acknowledgments

The author is eternally grateful to those who helped so much and wants to recognize some of these:

1. Pastor Dwaine Lee and Pastor David Theobald for inspiration and encouragement.

2. William Hamilton for all the art which added vivid emphasis to the Bible truths.

3. To my secretaries: Rebecca Little, Vivian Trimble, Carol Sturgeon, and Judy Lund.

4. To Jan Hutka, my wife, who listened patiently, making many helpful suggestions.

5. To the Holy Spirit, for guidance and help.

BOOM OR BUSTED

MONEY PROBLEMS

MISUNDERSTANDING THE PURPOSE OF MONEY AND ITS EFFECT ON YOU AND YOUR FAMILY.

A business without a good budget generally is heading toward bankruptcy and a home without responsible money management often ends up in divorce or "a hell on earth."

There is much misunderstanding of the importance of money and its value to each of us. It has been called many uncomplimentary names such as "filthy lucre," "dirty money," and so on. However, it took money for you and me to have breakfast this morning, and to provide goods so that we can clothe ourselves. Without it we would soon perish from nakedness, cold, and starvation. When we realize that God provides this gift it soon begins to take on unprecedented importance.

Money is a very necessary ingredient in the successful existence of a family, but its misuse can be as fatal as gasoline. It can explode a marriage and dismember the whole family, leaving a life of wreckage.

You may ask, does not the Bible say money is evil? The answer is no, but it does say, "the love of money is the root of all evil" (1 Tim. 6:10). Now we must find out what constitutes this *love of money*.

Perhaps I can illustrate it this way. About two months ago I walked into the office of one of my tenants who runs a private

Does this person love food?

police company and weighs about 450 pounds. He was eating his lunch. On the desk was a pan about one foot wide, two feet long, and about three inches deep. It was filled with custard from which he was busily eating. But that was not all he had to eat. On the same desk were six other empty dishes and two empty milk cartons. If someone asked you if this man loves food, what would be your answer? It is obvious he loves food because he eats so much. Clearly this is a case of excessive consumption.

The individuals who spend (consume) all the money they can earn and borrow may perhaps be the ones who have the love of money which is the root of all evil. When money is used as God intended, it is one of the most valuable temporal gifts given to man. It will not only sustain him and his family but also it can be used to propagate the gospel to the lost world.

SERVANTS TO MONEY.

The borrower is servant to the lender. (Prov. 22:7)

The majority of families have a very difficult time resisting various credit cards, time purchases, and impulse buying which reduces the buying power and adds unplanned stress on the family. Soon a second job is required and it seems that a trap has sprung. So many hours are spent in working to make payments caused by unscrupulous covetousness for personal belongings that there isn't time to enjoy the items purchased. Then it happens—the fatigue and disillusionment known as the "rat race" mounts up and the pace speeds up toward the unavoidable crises. Screams and accusations can be heard. "Why did you buy this?!"; "Money! Money! That is all I hear!" Things get out of control.

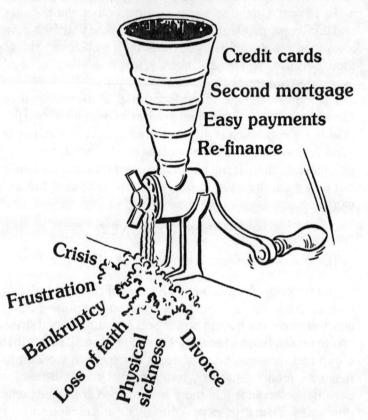

WAGES

Credit cards
Second mortgage
Easy payments
Re-finance

Crisis
Frustration
Bankruptcy
Loss of faith
Physical sickness
Divorce

Eliminate the money grinder and begin to prosper. From Romans 13:8

IRRESPONSIBLE USE OF OUR RESOURCES.

Christ was very explicit in teaching that the one who uses his limited resources properly will be given more. When the same resources are misused, on the other hand, that little bit will be taken from him. This is a very important principle. It is confirmed by the Parable of the Pounds (Luke 19:11-27) and the Parable of the Talents (Matt. 25:14-30).

If you find yourself in serious financial circumstances cheer up, for there is hope. God's Word contains clear and understandable principles which we will be discussing and illustrating as we go along in this book. These principles show you how to get out of debt and be blessed by God more than you have dreamed possible and also have money to give to the needy.

As a general rule, a business without a good budget generally is heading toward bankruptcy and a home without responsible money management often ends up in divorce or "a hell on earth," with unresolved stress and resentment.

Over the past eight to ten years many businessmen operating small businesses have come to me for counseling. Included in this group were men with master's degrees in mathematics, even some accountants. The one common element was that they were not disciplined. They were going along hoping circumstances would somehow work out. They generally do—in the form of disaster.

A high school teacher I know wanted to capitalize on his talent in upholstering. He was a brilliant and capable person. He invested all his life's savings and also his sister's savings in an upholstering business. One day he brought his books to me to evaluate. He was hoping that by increasing production

5

of one more divan a week he could possibly make money, but his records showed a loss of more than fifty thousand dollars in the previous year. He did not have a realistic budget. He displayed his merchandise in the best showroom on the West Coast, and was making a good product; yet he was failing financially. Being an optimistic fellow he continued hoping that somehow it would all work out.

All businessmen should know that there are unforeseen costs in business known as "hidden costs." A family also has hidden costs that demand additional funds. Responsible parents know that circumstances don't always work out as planned and, therefore, they provide for unknown expenses by building reserves through systematic savings.

A dear friend of mine was laid off. With his job went his family health insurance and other benefits. Being the father of five boys, he didn't seem to be able to accumulate a savings. Instead, he seemed to always be in debt. One day one of his teen-age boys had a motorcycle accident in which two bones of the right leg were broken about six inches below the knee. This unanticipated tragedy required hospitalization for several days and the bill amounted to over $1,000. The father found himself in even greater debt. How different the outcome could have been if he had planned for hidden costs.

In 1970 my wife and I took a guided tour through seven countries in Europe. We visited Italy, Austria, Switzerland, France, the Netherlands, and England. We were with a group of schoolteachers. I was interested in watching our teacher friends as our bus would stop at the various souvenir shops. These people would rush from the bus to the shops buying all types of trinkets and stuffing their bags full. This pattern was consistent for the first few days of the tour, but soon some of these same shoppers exceeded their funds and had to borrow from others to pay for their food. Some sold their souvenirs at a fraction of the price they had previously paid. These were grown, educated, but financially irresponsible, people.

Your scholastic accomplishments will not necessarily make you a good manager of the family finances. Often on the contrary, the feeling that you consider yourself better educated than the average can in itself become a mental block. You can prove this to yourself by trying to borrow money from the local bank simply on the basis of a master's or a PhD degree. The results will surprise you. You may see an immigrant, with his son helping him with English, walking out with a large loan given by a loan officer who is more impressed by the immigrant's ability to manage money than with your scholastic accomplishments.

DOES MONEY BUY HAPPINESS?

If money can buy happiness then why is it that many of the rich commit suicide? In 1921 nine of the most successful money-making men got together at the Edgewater Hotel in Chicago. They included the head of one of the largest monopolies, a successful Wall Street speculator, the president of the largest utility of that time, the president of the largest steel company, the president of the Bank of International Settlements and a member of the U.S. president's cabinet. (Their activities became known later as the Teapot Dome Scandal.)

What had happened to these men twenty-five years later who had possessed this fantastic power previously? Let us take a look. Iven Kruger, suicide; Jessie Livermore, suicide;

Charles Schwab, lived in bankruptcy; Samuel Insull, died a fugitive from justice and penniless; Howard Hopkins, went insane; Arthur Cotton, bankrupt; Richard Whitney, president of the New York Stock Exchange, was released finally from Sing Sing Penitentiary; Leon Frasier, suicide; and Albert Fall, released from prison so he could die at home.

Several years ago, a Gallup Poll reported that a review of the people who found happiness in life were not the craftsmen whose jobs were protected by unions nor the rich nor the person with the secure job but the devoutly religious people. Jesus said, "My peace I give unto you: not as the world giveth, give I unto you" (John 14:27).

2

IS IT A SIN TO BE RICH?

Sin is a subject which has been given hundreds of definitions. Therefore, one more will not be out of order. This definition is based on the Scriptures.

And God said, Let us make man in our image, after our likeness. (Gen. 1:26)

Why did God make man in His own likeness? Could it be so He could have companionship and fellowship with man? Then can it be that "sin" has been defined so simply that we have overlooked its real meaning? Sin is simply anything which hampers the purpose for which God created us; it is anything that breaks the companionship. If this is so, then we may ask, does our money enhance this companionship or distract us from it? If it enhances it, then money is a blessing and you can be trusted with prosperity. If it hinders then it is a sin to you.

Some of the greatest men of God were rich: "Abraham was very rich in cattle, in silver and in gold" (Gen. 13:2). Solomon was given both riches and honor by God (1 Chron. 29:12). Job was mightily blessed (Job 42:12), and the children of Israel were told, "But thou shalt remember the Lord thy God: for it is he that giveth thee power to get wealth" (Deut. 8:18).

Now to really answer the question, "Is it a sin to be rich?" The answer depends on you. "Where your treasure is, there will your heart be also" (Luke 12:34). If you treasure your riches above your fellowship with your Savior Jesus Christ then to you it is a sin, but if God blesses you in such a way that He will get the glory from your riches, it is not a sin for you to be rich; in fact, your riches can and will be used to the glory of God by spreading the good news of the saving power of Jesus Christ.

For years I struggled in California as an electrical contractor. At one time I employed sixty-five electricians. I literally ran from job to job and worked so hard that on many nights it would be midnight or after by the time I would return home. Frequently I would not even stop for dinner because I was preparing bids. The reward for all this relentless work and time often was a loss of the contract because we were not the low bidder and the award went to someone else.

Is It a Sin to Be Rich?

I remember working consistently over seventy hours a week doing millions of dollars worth of electrical work, but at the end of each year something unforeseen always happened which siphoned off the expected profits. All during this time I attended church, paid my tithes faithfully, and participated as a board member. I was also a Sunday school teacher, but when it came right down to it I reaped exactly what I sowed. It was eighteen years of frustration and pressure. Soon my health began to give way. My over-taxed nerves gave me an attack of hives two or three times a day and I had many sleepless nights. I felt ready to climb the walls; it was truly a hell on earth. I understood why men's hearts could fail because of failing in business.

All bills were paid but very little was left. I remember one of my secretaries said to me one day, "I have never seen so much money go through a place so fast without any of it sticking to the walls." Finally the doctor said to me, "You want to live? Then quit business and get an easy job like operating an elevator."

"Me!! The president of the Northern California Electrical Contractors' Association? Never! I'll keep the hives three times a day and a stomach ulcer."

But it did not take long until I was willing to say, "Yes, Lord. Anything you want me to be I will be." From there on I shifted my focus and God began to work in my heart. In fact, He gave me a new heart. Now nothing seemed to matter more than communion with the Master.

Later, on one occasion I was reviewing the finances of my company with Jerry, my certified public accountant. I was complaining about the county assessor's appraisal of $125,000 for the building I shared with three other tenants.

God was speaking to me through Jerry, for now I was beginning to listen to any source God wanted to use. Since God had spoken to a prophet through the mouth of a donkey, to Moses through a burning bush, and Belshazzar with writing on the wall I guess it was as if he wanted to speak to me through a C.P.A. It was like a voice of assurance within my heart.

After finishing my complaint, Jerry said to me, "You know, Ed, the assessor is probably right about the value of your property. Besides, this is the only thing I see that made any money for you and if you want to see a fool go look in a mirror. For while you were running yourself ragged, your three tenants were paying for this building. Quit bitching about the only thing which is paying off!" What a rebuke! It was not like Jerry. He was normally very diplomatic. He advised me to get out of the electrical business and become a landlord. Believe it or not, only six years later, someone accused me of being the largest individual landlord in my hometown of 50,000 people, and, at the same time, I was spending half of my time as a Christian layman ministering with Full Gospel Business Men, Christian radio broadcasting, prison ministries, and counseling. Soon I was attending several prayer luncheons and prayer breakfasts weekly and even making several missionary trips lasting as many as thirty days in foreign countries. One of these trips was behind the Iron Curtain. What made the difference? My emphasis was not on money but on the kingdom of God. "Seek ye first the kingdom of God, and his righteousness; and all these things shall be added unto you" (Matt. 6:33). After putting my priorities in the correct order God gave me a keen awareness of His will and made me capable of making the right decisions as His steward.

I could tell you stories you may find hard to believe about how God blessed. Did I just lie down and let God do it all? No, I continued to be fervent in business, but the greatest joy I have found is leading a soul to Christ. In fact, this means more to me than acquiring the most wealthy tenant or constructing the largest building in my town.

3

TITHING AND
GOD'S PROMISES

"Bring ye all the tithes into the storehouse, that there may be meat in mine house, and prove me now herewith, saith the Lord of hosts, if I will not open you the windows of heaven, and pour you out a blessing, that there shall not be room enough to receive it. And I will rebuke the devourer for your sakes, and he shall not destroy the fruits of your ground; neither shall your vine cast her fruit before the time in the field, saith the Lord of hosts" (Mal. 3:10, 11).

WHY DO I STILL HAVE FINANCIAL PROBLEMS THOUGH I TITHE FAITHFULLY?

Many Christians ask this question. Jesus spoke to this question very carefully in the parable of the talents and the pounds. One person was not a good steward (manager) of the money given to him and therefore even what he had was taken away and given to those who had many talents.

As you continue to read this book you soon will be aware that those who overspend will find that the more God blesses them the more they suffer and instead of getting better their financial situation only gets worse.

The question is often asked, how much money is enough for me to live on comfortably? That is a relative question. Consider the masses in India who look at the people in China and say, "The Chinese are rich." And by India's standards they are.

Yet the Chinese think they are poor in comparison to the Russians. And they say, "The Russians are rich."

The Russians say, "We are not rich; the French are rich."

The French say, "The Americans are rich."

So it is Americans they are talking about—the richest people on earth. We are at least five or six rungs higher on the financial ladder than the Indians. Therefore, why do you and your next-door neighbor still have financial problems? Surely it is poor management. You will be astounded to find out how easy it would be for you to actually become a millionaire by just changing your priorities in your lifetime. Hundreds of people in America are doing it every year because they have learned the law of saving, sowing, and reaping spoken of so much in the Bible.

Many Americans have a passion to overspend and the result is that the more they earn the more they overspend, creating a vicious cycle.

It must be very *frustrating* to God. For if God gives this type of a family $1,000 a month in wages they generally overspend 10 percent and are $100 behind every month. Should God give them $2,000 a month with the probability that they will continue overspending 10 percent, causing them to go into debt $200 a month? Therefore, the consequence is that the more God blesses them, the more they hurt.

There are many devastating habits like gluttony and too much alcohol. The pattern is the same. The more one drinks the more he wants to drink; the more he eats the more he wants to eat. You may say I am glad I am not an alcoholic, or a glutton, but are you a "spendaholic"? The pattern is the same in this addiction, leading to financial disaster that not only hurts you but also your family and acquaintances.

Several years ago I had a secretary who was in her late thirties whose husband had a good job at a local technical laboratory. Her mother lived with them and paid room and board. This secretary was paid a salary equal to construction workers, considerably more than other secretaries. The combined salary of this lady and her husband was far above the average and yet they always seemed to have trouble making ends meet. They were not known to drink; neither did they travel. The only sports they participated in was bowling once a week. What was wrong? Others seemed to make out much better on half their salary.

Let us look at their spending habits. They seemed to be buying new things—a deep freezer with wrapped meat, water softener, four-wheel drive vehicle which never left the pavement, waterbeds, and on and on. All of these were bought on time. Often the interest is a much as 18 percent on such a payment plan. I remember how she would tell about the large savings they made by making these purchases, repeating the claim made by the salesman, "It's a good deal." One Christmas season she was crying because their complete income was allocated to monthly payments and she had no money to purchase Christmas gifts. One consequence of purchasing beyond their means was having to assign and consolidate their bills in order to keep their purchases. After the one big single monthly payment was paid, there simply wasn't any money left.

God always very carefully works out a plan for man. The children of Israel were blessed by God, but they had to live by His principles, even though He could have performed a miracle and rained down wheat on the children of Israel as He did manna in the desert. He wanted them to live by the law of harvest.

THE LAW OF HARVEST

Be not deceived, God is not mocked; for whatsoever a man soweth, that shall he also reap. (Gal. 6:7)

Isn't it true that if you sow nothing you also reap nothing? But God promises to bless the increase of your land. The children of Israel, after gathering their grain, had to save enough seed to plant the next crop or there would be no next crop no matter how much they gave to the priests. In Proverbs we read the Scripture: "Go to the ant, thou sluggard [irresponsible person]; consider her ways, and be wise: Which having no guide, overseer, or ruler, Provideth her meat in the summer, and gathereth her food in the harvest. How long wilt thou sleep, O sluggard? when wilt thou arise out of thy sleep? Yet a little sleep, a little slumber, a little folding of the hands to sleep: So shall thy poverty come as one that travelleth, and thy want as an armed man'' (Prov. 6:6-11).

Following a harvest a certain Jewish farmer had ten bags of grain. As a good follower of the commandments of God he gave the Levites one bag. Then he had nine. He could have used all nine for himself; instead, he sat one bag aside for seed and another bag for an insurance against drought. It was imperative for him to save a portion of his crop and to plant it so God would multiply it.

The educational system in our country has played a vital role in the growth and progress of America and statistics will confirm that those who have a good education are paid higher wages. And those who have graduated from a college or a university have many more opportunities for employment. However, within our educational system no one has provided a means to communicate God's financial principles to the students.

Blessed is the man that walketh not in the counsel of the ungodly . . . But his delight is in the law of the Lord; . . . he shall be like a tree planted by the rivers of water, that bringeth forth his fruit in his season; his leaf also shall not wither; and whatsoever he doeth shall prosper. The ungodly are not so: they are like the chaff which the wind driveth away. (Ps. 1:1-3)

In Bible times they did not have machinery to harvest and

thresh the barley or wheat. Therefore, they had to do it manually. The process of separating the grain from the stalk and husk was known as threshing. This threshing took place on a flat surface of stone large enough to hold the bundles for beating with sticks to crumble the straw and the husk. This crumbled straw and the husks were called chaff and it was not usable for food.

Christ gave this answer: "Thou shalt not tempt the Lord thy God" (Luke 4:12).

Credit buying of anything except real estate will cause servitude to the lender thus diminishing your dependence on God as your source.

The Law of Harvest

Let us consider the farmer who had a large amount of the finest equipment money could buy. With this equipment he could plow, subsoil, and even harvest. He had thousands of acres of the finest land. If he actually did not plant any seed, he surely would have no crop to harvest.

Many Christians can be compared to this farmer. They work hard. In fact, they get up early and work until it is very late. They often work on more than one job. In spite of all of this work they continue to have tremendous difficulties making ends meet. This is because they have saved no seed money for God to multiply. Their compulsive buying on time has stolen hundreds of dollars of *seed money* each month from their family budget, leaving their fields totally barren at harvest time.

Christian, if seed is not sown God has nothing to multiply. If you will save seed money, and plant it with God's direction, it will multiply in unbelievable ways.

Only the grain was used as the principal ingredient in making bread. To use this grain it had to be separated from the chaff. This separation could be accomplished by putting the beaten chaff and grain into a flat basket which was so large that two people were required to handle it. During a brisk wind they would move the basket up and down in an action similar to that of a trampoline. The chaff and grain would be tossed into the air. The chaff, being much lighter, would be blown away by the wind. The grain would drop back into the basket completely separated and ready to be ground into flour.

If someone follows the world system of finance they will be like the chaff, having no stability and heading toward financial chaos.

You may suspect that the writer of this book is against the world's system of credit. May I suggest that God is also? The clever schemes which tempt you to raise your standard of spending above God's provision can be compared to Satan's temptation of Christ when he asked Jesus to jump off the pinnacle of the Temple. Satan said, "If thou be the Son of God, cast thyself down from hence: For it is written, He shall give his angels charge over thee, to keep thee: And in their hands they shall bear thee up, lest at any time thou dash thy foot against a stone" (Luke 4:9-11).

The world system is full of charlatans who are ready to rip the Christian off and have him tempt God. They misquote Scripture, saying that purchasing on time is an act of faith, but they say nothing about the high interest rates that constitute usury.

GETTING YOUR
PRIORITIES ORGANIZED

Unless the Lord builds the house,
    its builders will have toiled in vain.
Unless the Lord keeps watch over a city,
    in vain the watchman stands on guard.
In vain you rise up early
    and go late to rest,
toiling for the bread you eat;
    he supplies the need of those he loves.
Sons are a gift from the Lord
    and children a reward from him. (Ps. 127:1-3, NEB)

The family unit was established when God made Eve from and for Adam. This family was established more than four thousand years before the church began. In fact, the church as it is known today is a very recent creation. In spite of this, some put the church in the first place and the family in the last place, thinking that somehow the church is more holy than the home. I have known many folks who rush from work to church, not giving sufficient time for their children.

The church plays a very important role in helping the family, especially when all the family members attend church together. If you have small children or are contemplating starting your family, begin attending church now, and the chances are your children will continue to attend as they get older. Remember, however, that the church will not raise your family for you. That responsibility and opportunity rests with the parents. No one but the parents can do it.

I've often wondered about the effect of only two people and how far their influence reaches. Let us look at one case.

Several years ago I began to draw up a family tree of my grandparents and their descendants. My grandparents, on my father's side, emigrated from Czechoslovakia approximately 100 years ago. I was amazed to find out that today there are 200 descendants from this one couple. At this same rate of growth, in another 100 years this family could grow to 20,000—enough for a small city. Wow! What an effect—spiritually, financially, and socially—two people have. We know that God's punishment reaches to the third and fourth generation (Deut. 5:9). This means as many as a thousand people may be affected by a single life.

"The wise man looks ahead. The fool attempts to fool himself and won't face facts" (Prov. 14:8 TLB).

Some want to unite the family, but continue to put it off until things change.

"If you wait for perfect conditions, you will never get anything done" (Eccles. 11:5 TLB).

Many active Christian parents think only about their own need of fellowship. They will participate in every type of meeting and yet somehow they are strangers to their own children who have an even greater need of fellowship and love. Children will naturally look to their parents for love and acceptance. If mom and dad are gone, frequently seeking their own fulfillment and short-changing their children, the kids will soon look elsewhere for relationships. When these immature children turn to their friends who also have the same problems, they frequently begin to experiment with life, often destroying their moral and spiritual values. Soon they become caught in a web of life they cannot understand. The drug community is waiting to send them on their way to crime, prison, or death. Crying and prayers often come too late.

Mom and dad, may I invite you to visit Soledad Prison with us and see what parental neglect of children has fostered? Many young men are at the mercy of hardened sex perverts who, with their power of persuasion, take away the last vestige of dignity from these youths. Sure, we have glowing testimonies of how two or three are miraculously delivered every month. However, hundreds are still lost to this life as well as eternity.

Perhaps the priorities could be summarized in this order:

First: Your relationship and loyalty to God.

Second: Your relationship and loyalty to your family—spiritually, financially, socially, and mentally.

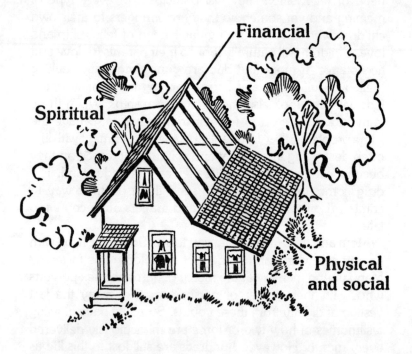

Is your financial roof missing for the protection of your family?

Third: Your relationship to your fellow man.

Fourth: Your relationship to your church and community.

If you have these priorities reversed, you will encounter spiritual and mental difficulties. "There is a way which seemeth right unto a man, but the end thereof, are the ways of death" (Prov. 14:12).

Your heart would break if you knew the deplorable conditions found in many homes I have visited. The parents are too busy doing their own thing to attend to the needs of their children as they are growing up. After the age for training is over many come in for counseling. A short and simple review of the children's activities generally gives obvious proof of why the children are lost.

Thank God, there are still millions of happy Christian homes with children who have good relationships with their parents and God. They are the only hope for the future.

Americans can be lost in the home instead of on the foreign battlefield. This country is full of POWs from the battles which have taken place in the home.

One cannot concentrate on only one or two of these priorities by saying they are so important that there is no time for the others. Appropriate attention must be given to all.

On one occasion a man was planning to build a home on a Pacific island. He had the lumber, the windows, the shingles, the paint, the plumbing—everything he needed except one thing: the nails. All this material became useless and had very little value because the house could not be fastened together without nails. In the same fashion a family unit with any one of the ingredients missing will suffer irreparable damage whether it be in the spiritual, financial, social, physical, or mental areas. It always takes your time, careful attention, and the help of God to raise a strong and healthy family. Raising a Christian family can be fun and very fulfilling.

The fun families have together cannot be purchased in any resort or hotel from Miami to Taipei. Our children reminisce about the Sunday afternoon trips to the river where we had picnics and skipped rocks on the water, but no one reminisces about trips to fancy restaurants which often cost as much for one meal as the grocery bill for the whole week.

For seven years we were privileged to spend a whole week each Easter season on Shasta Lake, camping and fishing with my daughter and her husband who have five boys in school. This was not a fancy deal but we enjoyed every minute of it. Some would fly kites, while others would build a fireplace of rocks for the evening bonfire. We laughed, played, and enjoyed each other. This became the greatest week in each year. We talk about the fun we had. We often reminisce about the occasion when one child fell into the cold lake or snapped a fishing pole in two when he thought he had a big fish, only to find it was caught on a snag on the bottom. Sometimes the smallest person caught the biggest fish. Our picture albums are full of exciting remembrances. These were great times.

Whole families need to go together on outings. Sometimes more damage is done by splitting the family than by not going at all. Of course, carefully considered exceptions can be made.

My son attended a woodworking class in high school. One day he brought a classmate to our house. During the course of discussion this boy commented that his father never did anything with him. Although this boy was in high school he had never driven a nail and did not know what the hammer was for nor how to use it properly. He was very hungry for a sense of identification; however, his dad just did not have any time for his most precious possession: *his son*.

Bill Gothard conducts seminars throughout America. When he came to Oakland, California, the attendance was so great that the large sports coliseum was filled with people. His presentation was also beamed to neighboring cities by closed-circuit television. People flock to hear him, coming by train, cars, and hundreds of chartered or private buses.

The name of the seminar is "The Institute in Basic Youth Conflicts." May we suggest that you watch for it in your area? Go, and take your children with you. This institute was conducted each night for a week and all day on Friday and Saturday. It has been more effective in uniting families spiritually, mentally, and socially, than anything I have ever experienced.

Young people struggling to accept parents and parents struggling to accept their children began to understand each other and get it all together. The parents benefited as much as the young people.

Bill describes the function of the family unit which he calls the "chain of command." God first, father second, mother third, the children fourth. God is pictured as the great and all-knowing force, the father is the motivator or the hammer, the mother is the cutting chisel and the teen-ager is the diamond which is being cut and shaped. He supports everything by Scriptures.

Find out when the seminar will be held in your area and plan to attend, even if you have to work it into your vacation. The teens will love it and mom and dad will sit engrossed by the practical biblical truths being revealed.

**The father is very important
in protecting the family**

Another illustration Bill uses shows the father as the umbrella over the family. The wife is portrayed as the umbrella's framework supporting the father and protecting the children. When the umbrella is not there, leaving only the handle and framework, the children are much more exposed to the influence of Satan. When the umbrella is stretched out and held in place the children are isolated from Satan. If there are holes in the umbrella, then Satan can and often does penetrate the family unit.

Principles of Family Finance:
A. To provide basic needs for food and clothing.
B. God wants to demonstrate His power. If you buy on credit, you limit God.
C. Results of *credit buying of depreciating goods.* (Such as cars, boats, recreational vehicles, etc.)
   1. It is not scriptural. "Owe no man any thing, but to love one another" (Rom. 13:8).
   2. It brings bondage. "The rich ruleth over the poor, and the borrower is servant to the lender" (Prov. 22:7).
   3. It involves presumption about the future. "Go to now, ye that say, To day or tomorrow we will go into such a city, and continue there a year, and buy and sell, and get gain: Whereas ye know not what shall be on the morrow. For what is your life? It is even a vapour, that appeareth for a little time, then vanisheth away. For that ye ought to say, If the Lord will, we shall live, and do this, or that. But now ye rejoice in your boastings: all such rejoicing is evil. Therefore to him that knoweth to do good, and doeth it not, to him it is sin" (James 4:13-17).

AMERICA, A LAND
OF OPPORTUNITY

Before the turn of the century many people in Europe, tied down by oppression, immigrated to America. Like many Americans, my father and his parents were among those who came to these shores almost 100 years ago from Czechoslovakia, which at the time was under the rule of Austria. A few years ago I had the privilege of visiting the homeland of my father. I saw the church and school he attended and even the house where he once lived. Some of my distant kin reviewed the history which was full of catastrophies such as hunger and oppression which, in reality, have never stopped. Continuously, they have been under oppressive regimes, from Kaiser Wilhelm to Hitler and now the Communists. I was made to realize, by contrast, the opportunities afforded in America. Included in the many freedoms we enjoy is the ability to own real estate. The common man cannot only own property, but he can become rich if he applies the law of harvest spoken so much about in the Scriptures. This makes seed money available to be multiplied by the principles set down by God instead of spending it all under an impulse to buy.

The opportunities for financial success are greater now than ever in America as we can see if we look at the vast holdings of common working people everywhere who have learned to be conservative in their affairs and willing to be good stewards. God seems to bless Christians and sinners alike who will live according to His laws.

Imagine the son of an immigrant, after learning the principle of God's harvest, being accused of being "the largest property owner in his town." This has to be the land of opportunity. In what other country could a peanut farmer who had the aid of a Small Business Administration loan, operating a peanut farm and warehouse, become the president of that nation? This is truly the greatest nation in the world.

An immigrant from Italy applied the principle: "The borrower is a servant of the lender" (Prov. 22:7) and became the president of the Bank of Italy, later called the Bank of America, the world's largest bank.

In what other country can you purchase income property with 20 percent down and have the tenant pay you more than it costs to pay it off?

It is well known that if California were made an

independent nation, it would be the world's fifth richest nation. It exports more food to other nations than they individually produce. I have found fruit from California everywhere I have traveled, even in Czechoslovakia. God's abundance is everywhere and yet some say, "What can I do? Don't you know I am just a poor wage earner?"

Moses was only a sheepherder with a dried-up, crooked stick in his hand, but he led 3,000,000 people. When God first spoke to Moses, He asked him, "What is in thine hand?"

"A rod," was the reply. And this was the stick God used to lead a whole nation. Let us not limit God by looking at the stick, let's look unto the eternal flame of God who is refining the gold He is making for His people.

Have you been fishing all your life and caught nothing but frustration? Cast your net on the right side where God can fill it until it begins to burst.

AWAKE, CHRISTIANS! Discipline your spending and possess the land God is giving you. Do you see giant, walled cities or are you a victim of having finances as your master? Is your job your source? Let God be your source. He will tumble down the walls.

TURN AROUND
(FIVE STEPS NEEDED)

The question is often asked, "How can I get out of the financial mess I have gotten myself into?" The answer stresses effort and determination.

You may ask, "Why doesn't God rain money down from heaven and solve my problems?" The truth is that financial problems of most people are not solved by an additional supply of money, because they are caused by the lack of knowledge and discipline in management. Therefore, it is better for you if God allows you to learn to manage and then to walk out of the financial mess step by step. This process will allow you to understand the mistakes you made getting into the mess so the same mistakes are not repeated in the future. The journey out of your financial mess must start with a "turnaround," consisting of five steps:

1. Make God the *director* of your finances as well as the *supplier*.
2. Avoid credit card misuse.
3. Pay cash for all purchases except real estate.
4. Receive consent from God and your spouse for all substantial purchases.
5. Save seed money.

Now let's consider each step:

1. MAKE GOD THE DIRECTOR OF YOUR FINANCES AS WELL AS THE SUPPLIER.

Many Christians view God as one they must continually come to and beg for their daily provision which by their own confession makes them beggars instead of sons and daughters.

I have noticed with interest the concern of many about how the church offerings are spent. They will spend hours arguing with great concern over a small sum and pay little attention to the method they use in spending the earnings they have asked God to give them through their jobs. What we are really saying is that we must realize that *everything* we receive is really God's and that we are only the stewards. When this change of attitude begins to take place, Christians begin to be blessed and have taken the first step on their way out of the financial mess.

2. AVOID CREDIT CARD MISUSE.

Each time you have to "spread out" your payment on any

credit card purchase you will pay 18 percent interest or even more on the unpaid balance. This type of interest has a devastating effect on the family budget.

Bob and Beth came to me after a church lecture on this subject and stated that they were in such a mess, and they could see no way out. I asked them if they had made credit card purchases and they stated that they had. I suggested they should have a credit card burning party when they got home and begin to trust God to meet their daily needs as they arise. Three weeks later when I returned to continue the series, Bob and Beth met me at the door. I noticed a gleam in their eyes as they related how after burning their credit cards they have already paid off three accounts and with excitement stated their new assurance that they could make it now without going through bankruptcy.

3. PAY CASH FOR ALL PURCHASES EXCEPT REAL ESTATE.

You will be pleasantly surprised as you implement a "cash only" policy and see how much farther your money will go. By taking a week longer to shop for an item you will find bargains you would not have seen if purchased earlier. Gasoline is often 10 to 15 percent cheaper in stations that sell for cash only. Recently, I shopped at a health store where a 5 percent discount is given when credit cards are not used. When you purchase a car for cash you can offer the dealer as much as 15 percent less than the asking price and generally he will take it.

Perhaps I should mention that many unnecessary items are purchased with credit cards because psychologically it seems that you are not really spending any money at the time. However, the realization hits when the mailman brings the bill.

We have excluded real estate from cash items because real estate is one commodity which has on the whole increased in value since the Pilgrims landed. This has been true throughout American history except for "The Great Depression" during the late 1920s. The only warning we make is that you should not buy a larger home than you can afford, for that may rob your family of other more essential needs.

SOMETHING SPECTACULAR TAKES PLACE WHEN YOU PURCHASE WITH CASH.

(1) *Excitement.*

There is an excitement which takes place when you buy on a cash-only basis. The anticipation builds all during the time you save the money for that moment. This feeling can be compared to a trip to Europe my wife and I made in 1970. We picked out what we considered to be the best plan. It included London, Paris, Vienna, and Rome and a highlight was the Passion Play in Upper Bavaria in the city of Oberammergau. This story of Christ has been acted out every ten years during summer months for the past several hundred years except during Hitler's reign in 1940. This play is put on by the people of the small town. Each town member lives with the hope that they may some day be chosen by the council as being the most likely to play the part of Mary, Joseph, John the Baptist, a disciple or possibly even the most honored role, Jesus.

This play was first done in a meadow in 1634 as a result of

the devastating black plague which ravaged Europe periodically several centuries ago. During the plagues as much as 20 percent of the population would be periodically wiped out. After death from this disease the body turns black. In Vienna you can visit the mass graves under the cathedral where victims of the black plague are buried.

When these plagues would strike, each community would try to isolate itself. Royalty might take a ship away from the continent. Cities would post guards and not allow anyone to enter. In fact, they would use bows and arrows to shoot anyone who would attempt to do so.

Oberammergau was such a village. Some of its own men were in the woods when the news of this plague reached the city and fear and panic gripped the town. Guards were posted and roadblocks were established. Orders were given to shoot even one's own neighbor if he tried to re-enter the city. Every traveler was suspected of carrying the germs of the plague and if he were allowed to enter the town, it could be wiped out.

News came that one night during the plague the men from the city who were out hunting slipped undetected into their homes during the darkness. Nothing now could save the village except prayer. So pray they did. They were impressed with God's promise to spare them, provided they would tell the world the story of Christ. They vowed to do this through the means of a day-long play. This play is given four days a week during the summer months of every tenth year and in this way hundreds of thousands attend and hear about Jesus.

Oberammergau has no hotels. Instead of turning visitors away, they are invited to stay in the homes of the townsfolk. What an exciting experience I had when I was embraced by an eighty-year-old German lady with tears in her eyes. She did not know a word of English, and we did not know German, but our spirits spoke a language of love.

Many of our church friends have said, "You are lucky to get to go." Yes, we were. However, with a little reform these same friends might have observed that they paid more interest and carrying charges than our trip cost. It was one of the bonuses we get for purchasing with cash, but what is more exciting, we have been enjoying a similar bonus each year ever since.

One of the major contributing factors toward getting the most from your resources is a good cash purchasing plan.

(2) *Spiritual changes.*

Faith and confidence in God are perhaps the most valuable psychological and spiritual changes that result from following this principle. Instead of crying and begging God to help you make the payments you will praise Him for giving you the necessities of life, without encumbering yourself with items of marginal value.

(3) *Physical changes.*

It is very interesting to observe one's appearance when he is in a financial mess. His countenance reveals worry and anxiety. The color in his face is often pale. He may experience headaches or ulcers and frequently during the interview he may have to swallow antacid pills. All of this comes from worrying about the future. Physical healing can be augmented by sound financial management.

4. RECEIVE CONSENT FROM GOD AND YOUR SPOUSE FOR ALL SUBSTANTIAL PURCHASES.

If you have difficulty conversing with either your spouse or God, a turnaround will be more difficult for you. Be on speaking terms with both; it pays great dividends.

If it sounds strange or difficult for you to comprehend the idea of getting consent from God or how to know what God is telling you, be assured that thousands, if not millions, of people from all walks of life actually talk with God. I was always interested in knowing just what transpired when God talked to Abraham. There is a record of this: "Now the Lord had said unto Abram, Get thee out of thy country, and from thy kindred, and from thy father's house, unto a land that I will shew thee: And I will make of thee a great nation, and I will bless thee, and make thy name great; and thou shalt be a blessing: And I will bless them that bless thee, and curse him that curseth thee: and in thee shall all families of the earth be blessed" (Gen. 12:1-3).

There were times when God spoke to Abraham by sending angels to talk to him. Sometimes he spoke to him through a dream. But when God called him to make the greatest decision of his life, the Bible simply states, "the Lord had said to Abraham."

It was at another time when God put the greatest test on Abraham's life by asking him to sacrifice Isaac. Again, the only record we have is that a conversation between God and Abraham had taken place and nothing is said about visions, dreams, or angels.

Abraham was over 100 years old when Isaac was born, and being his true heir, Abraham loved him very much. They surely played together and Abraham did not mind playing the children's games of that day. We read about God's

request in Genesis 22:1-2 in *The Living Bible.* Here we see
how God tested Abraham's faith and obedience.

"Abraham," God called.

"Yes, Lord?" he replied.

"Take with you your only son—yes, Isaac whom you love
so much—and go to the land of Moriah and sacrifice him
there as a burnt offering upon one of the mountains which I'll
point out to you!" Again, the Bible does not record a dream,
vision, or the appearance of an angelic messenger.

People who begin to live in close communion with God
find that the fellowship with Him is even more effective than a
dream or vision. People who have such a close
communication will talk about their experiences with great
exuberance and a glow of joy on their faces.

Helen Martin, a wonderful Spirit-filled friend of mine, tells
the story of how God spoke to her. Helen had been a faithful
Catholic, who always attended Sunday Mass. She said her
prayers faithfully, and went to confession regularly.

Her husband, Dick, is an executive for the Bank of
America. They have four children. Helen and three of the
children had health problems which made their life together a
bit heavy.

In 1975, Dick and Helen Martin were in their mid-thirties
and lived in Pleasanton, California. Someone invited them to
attend a weekend couples' retreat known as a Cursillo. Helen
tells how God always seemed to be around but somewhat
remote. She suspected that He was always watching
everything she was doing wrong, perhaps to punish her. This
made her often uncomfortable and frustrated.

During this retreat an in-depth study of walking with God
was the topic. The idea of "walking with God" bothered

Helen and almost made her angry. She decided to have it out with God and to settle this issue once and for all. On that same day she went to the church, which she felt was the dwelling place of God. It was at night and the chapel was dark. But this did not matter to Helen because she was determined to find out if God really cared for her. For the first time in her life, she began to talk to God out loud. She said, "God, I know you are here somewhere and that you hear me and I want to ask you the reason why you continue pursuing me. Is it because you want to make me miserable? Why don't you leave me alone so I can have peace?"

Helen did not hear an audible voice. She did not have a dream or a vision. She did not see an angel. Nonetheless, God did speak to her in a most powerful way. You may say this does not make any sense. If she did not hear a voice, have a vision or a dream, in what other way could she have heard from God? Well, let's look at the results of that encounter with God. Helen's conversation with God was as spectacular as the one Abraham had, with a similarly profound effect.

Abraham became a changed person who displayed a charisma in his worship unlike the dejection felt by others who worshiped idols. His attitude toward others also changed to honesty and fairness not generally displayed in his day. To the surprise of his observers, he continued to prosper until he became one of the richest men of his day. In spite of his riches, his prime interest was worship to the unseen God.

Should you ever have a chance to meet Helen, you will have the thrill of your life. She will relate her experience something like this: "A sense of peace, and a spiritual warmth—a love which I never knew before—came over me. The guilt and all frustration were gone. I knew at that moment I was really ready for heaven and no longer was there any hate for anything in my heart." Something wonderful had taken place. No psychologist, training union, Sunday school, catechism or confession could have done this. Helen was a different person. Her mind and attitude were changed. She felt a light freedom about life and an unexplainable love for God instead of the fear and frustration she had known before. What really happened was that God spoke and Helen became a different person.

Beaming with the joy of God, Helen tells many neat things that have happened to her since that time. She is able to bake homemade bread even though she is allergic to wheat flour.

The exciting part is what she does with some of the bread she bakes. As soon as she takes the bread out of the oven, and the aroma is still rising from the loaf, she places it on a breadboard, covers it with a napkin and prays that God will show her who she had really baked it for. Then she gets in the car and drives down the street until God tells her to stop.

Visualize this sandy-haired, 115-pound woman with a grin from ear to ear holding this loaf of bread in one hand and ringing the doorbell of a stranger's house, when suddenly a lady with curlers in her hair, in her pajamas, opens the door.

"I am Helen Martin and I live in your neighborhood." Now the loaf of bread is about chest high between these two ladies and the aroma is wonderfully appetizing. Helen continues, "My hobby is baking homemade bread and I made a loaf for you." Soon the ladies are inside slicing this bread as Helen tells her story of how God laid it on her heart to bake this bread for this lady personally, and how she got started in this bread ministry, and her encounter with God. Many of these ladies are ministered to spiritually through Helen's obedience to the voice of God. Again, it was not a vision or a dream, but the voice of the Holy Spirit.

Several years ago Jan and I were struggling to get our daughter through the frustrating teen years. There arose the peer pressure of high school and community, which is generally in opposition to the forces of God. We discussed, argued, laughed, and even cried as we faced the issues of life head-on. Sometimes we seemed to find solutions. Other times, there seemed to be none. I remember always encouraging her to talk to God, because He had all the answers especially when she disagreed with us about the conclusion. I still remember the change which took place during her encounter with God more than twenty years ago and she has not been the same since. She explains it this way: "While I was praying and reading the Bible, I could sense God's presence in my bedroom and I was afraid to go to sleep for He might be gone when I awoke; however, I did fall asleep and in the morning God's presence had not left." Christ said, "I will never leave thee nor forsake thee" (Heb. 13:5).

There are great advantages at times for God to speak to us by His Spirit instead of speaking in a vision, dream, or even through an angel.

In November, 1965, I flew my Cessna 182 to Darby, Montana. On this occasion it was for elk hunting and relaxation instead of business. A big snowstorm had just blanketed that area, piling up the snow to a depth of two feet or more and the temperature dropped to thirty degrees below zero. The airport was small with no traffic control tower or snowplow to clear the runways. Having successfully bagged a nice bull elk, I wanted to leave with the 800 pounds of fresh meat aboard the plane before the powdered snow crusted, making departure impossible.

Starting an airplane engine in cold weather like this was a new experience for me; however, I had received some advice that I recalled. The oil had thickened until it was almost solid from the cold, making it almost impossible to crank the engine. We had drained the oil on my arrival. Before getting ready to leave I warmed the oil on a stove to about 150 degrees. The hot oil was then poured into the cold engine. With a booster battery and a few turns of the prop, the engine started.

After allowing the engine to warm up, I began to taxi down the runway. The tips of the prop were hitting into about one foot of the powdered snow, sending it flying in a cloud. In several trips down the runway the plane would accelerate to only about thirty miles an hour. (A speed of more than sixty miles an hour was required to get us airborne.) I decided to make several runs up and down the runway, leaving solid tracks for the wheels and reducing the depth of the snow with the propeller. After several trips over this same runway it was ready for the final try. I prepared with a final check-out of the right and left magnetos, the propeller angle, elevators, ailerons, and engine speed. Now I was ready for the attempt.

The plane began to roll. Soon the engine was barking sharply as the throttle was against the fire wall. The speed went to thirty-five, then forty-five, up to fifty-five and approaching sixty but no more. Mid-field was near the point at which the airplane had to become airborne or the takeoff would have to be aborted. Just when I was getting ready to pull the throttle back I rocked the elevators forward and backwards and the plane suddenly leaped into the clear air. What an exhilarating feeling I experienced as the Continental engine with its sharp tone, backed with strength and power, raised the heavy-laden plane into the clear Montana sky. Everything seemed to be right. All instruments read properly. The airfield that lay head was Boise, Idaho, which reported clear weather without any snow.

The snow-covered mountains looked so beautiful with trees protruding here and there. Smoke from chimneys of sparsely scattered houses and cabins was rising like large marble columns. In an hour the airfield in Boise was visible. The wind was calm and the sky was clear with unlimited visibility. The temperature was at thirty degrees and the runway was clear. I noticed the dry turf to the left of the runway which had frozen and turned a light brown.

After making the final approach, the wheels began to touch the two-mile-long concrete runway. Suddenly, I noticed the left tire smoking because the wheel was not turning. God said to me, "Give it power. Lift off the runway and land it on the turf." I did not know why but the turf had just enough frozen water on it to make it a perfect landing strip for a plane with a frozen wheel. I did what God told me to do. I pushed the throttle. It went in three-fourths of the way, and the plane raised up about two feet off the surface. As gracefully as any stunt pilot who might have planned this move I landed the plane on the turf. Had I continued on the hard runway only a few seconds longer I would have nosed over or ground looped. There was no time for dreams, visions, or a prayer meeting. But through the Spirit I did something that was not premeditated—something that I had never been trained for. Totally unrehearsed, God's instructions saved my life and delivered 800 pounds of fine elk meat as God's provision to my family. The steaks, chops, and roasts were excellent, baked under the skillful hands of Jan.

Talking to God brings many fulfilling experiences to a Christian. Communication with Him almost becomes a heaven on earth.

5. ALWAYS SAVE SEED MONEY.

This is a very important step which will logically follow when the other four have been taken. If you do not accomplish the first four steps, your savings will be offset by debts and you may be in a financial mess without realizing it.

Investing saved money allows it to multiply and compound. A good example of the great amount of growth by compounded interest involves an occasion when we purchased a 100-pound sack of bentemite clay in powdered form. This clay is used as a lubricant so that heavy high voltage cables can be pulled through underground conduits. I had no previous experience with this clay except that the specifications of the job I was doing called for its use. I poured the contents of the 100-pound sack into two five-gallon, empty paint buckets and began to add water. The clay began to expand over the top of the buckets, so I got two more buckets and divided the clay mixture again. This time I added more water, and the four buckets soon were again overflowing. I got more and more buckets until finally I had ten full buckets.

Seed money is perhaps one of the most overlooked and most important principles in God's Word. Without seed money which you must save yourself, God usually does not bless the family financially. We have provided a bar chart in this book illustrating how seed money will grow when 9 percent interest is received.

A few days ago a local newspaper carried the headlines: "Compounded Interest Makes Millionaires." The article spoke of how a few thousand invested in a savings account with compound interest and left there from twenty to thirty years multiplies to astronomical sums. The San Francisco newspaper carried a story of a lady who gave the city $1,000 in 1978 to be placed with a conventional banking institution and left to compound for ninety-nine years and four months at which time the city will receive one million dollars. (The agreement was sealed in a capsule.)

Read the incredible story by Bill Nickerson: "How I Made a Million Dollars in Real Estate in My Spare Time." Now his new edition says "Three Million." The story tells how he was working for the telephone company and how he and his wife lived in an apartment which they decided to clean up by painting. It looked so good the landlord raised their rent. This did not make Bill angry; rather he learned a principle here.

Just a few gallons of paint and a little work allowed the rent to be raised with a 100 percent return in the first year on the cost of the paint.

Bill and his wife said to each other, "This is our opportunity." They began saving some seed money and planning. Before long they made a down payment on a single-family home which needed painting and some repair. After doing the repairs they raised the price of the house more than 25 percent. They put it on the market and traded for a multiple (apartments) which had low rents because of the negligent care given by the former landlord. Again they painted and repaired, having all the work done by hired men and time after time they found the value of property could be raised more than the cost. They followed this pattern for ten years and became millionaires. Now they are telling others all over the country how easy it is to do, provided the seed money is saved in the first place and planted so God can multiply it.

One day there was a little boy who went to hear Jesus talk. His mom had prepared a lunch for him to take. She put five rolls and two fishes in his basket. Perhaps the boy got so interested in what Jesus was saying that he forgot to eat his lunch. He undoubtedly heard Jesus telling Philip and some of the other men to feed the huge crowd. Philip panicked and said, "It would take thousands of dollars to buy enough food for such a large crowd!"

The little boy told Philip that Jesus could have his lunch because He preached so hard and must be hungry. Philip took the lunch and gave it to Jesus. Even though Jesus took it He did not eat it. Instead, He told all the people to sit down in circles or groups. He began to break the rolls and fishes and fill huge baskets which the men helped carry into the crowd. The people ate and ate but none of the basekts seemed to get empty and after everybody had seconds and some even had thirds, Jesus said, "Pick up all that is left so nothing is wasted." After the disciples did what they were told, there were twelve huge basketfuls left.

What if one of the disciples had filled the little boy's basket with the leftovers? Let's presume they did and let's imagine what might have happened when the little boy got home. Let's follow the boy home.

"Mom! Mom! Where are you?"

"Don't scream, son. I hear you and I saw you coming.

What do you have in your basket? It's almost dragging the ground."

"That's just it, mom. You gave me two perch and five rolls." Snatching the lid open she could see that there were at least ten rolls and several fish.

"So you did not eat your lunch. In fact, it looks like it grew!"

"Mom, I did too. You know what I mean."

"Son, don't be so excited and calm down and tell me where you got these extra rolls."

"Mom, you never understand! Jesus made them multiply and if you don't believe it just look at the rolls. They all have the same kind of nicks you have in your bread pan."

The mother examined the rolls and, sure enough, they all had the signs of being baked in her own pan.

"Well, I'll be. They do. But, son, why did you break each of them? Don't you know they dry out faster?"

"Mom, that's just it. I did not break them. Jesus did."

"Well, if you say so, son. But why would a grown man do this?"

"Mom, there was this big crowd of people like at the yearly bazaar. You know, zillions of people!"

"Yes, son. Like four or five thousand?"

"And they had nothing to eat. The men were worried because some might get sick going all the way home without any food and I didn't want Jesus to get sick so I gave Him my lunch. Was it okay, mom?"

"That was nice of you, son, but why did He turn it down?"

"Mom, you never understand. He didn't turn it down. He took the bread and had all the people sit down in big circles. Then He looked up and said something. I couldn't hear Him, but I guess who He was talking to did hear him. Then He took the rolls and began to break them. Mom, it was so neat. Every time He broke an end off another one grew right on. He would put it into those huge baskets. And when all these zillions—"

"Thousands, son."

"Oh, mom, thousands. But it looked like zillions to me, and then all the crowd had seconds—some thirds—and I had fourths. I was really hungry. Was it okay?"

"Now, son, just tell me what happened."

"Well, Jesus said, 'Pick up all that is left over.' He called it 'remnants' so that nothing was wasted. Mom, when it was so easy for Him to make this bread, why bother saving what is left? It would be much easier to throw it away and make more."

"Son, Jesus must be a prophet because He knows God is very unhappy when we don't appreciate what He gives us by throwing some of it away just because it is easier to make something new."

"I see, mom, that is why daddy always saves those bags of barley and when we have more than we need he gives it to our neighbor."

"That is true and remember, son, if your father did not save seed and plant it we would not have fields of barley for our bread."

"I see, mom. Dad makes the barley multiply like Jesus did but it is not cooked."

"No, son. Your daddy only plants the seed and God multiplies it for him just like Jesus did."

FAMILY BUDGET

A lively discussion can usually be generated on the usefulness of a family budget, but have you ever seen a successful business without a good, detailed budget? I have concluded that a workable budget must be born from the motivation to accomplish a specific financial goal. There must be a goal in order for a goal to be reached. When you ask some people, "What is the financial goal for your family?" they will often reply, "To get by," and that is exactly what they get and often even less.

Records are a tool.
A family budget is a tool available to every family that strives to be successful; however, planning involves setting a goal.

In 1940, during the time when everyone was still feeling the effects of the 1929 Depression, money was not only scarce but almost nonexistent. Our first child was born in the county clinic in San Francisco. I suspected that the prenatal care might not be the best available. The feeling I had at that time prompted me to save 10 percent of all I earned in addition to tithing, and this became my first seed money. At that time I was earning eighty dollars per month, but God saw my purpose and not only did He multiply the eight dollars I saved but He gave me more in proportion to my ability to be trusted.

When I went into business, some eleven years later, this savings account had already multiplied to $22,000 in addition to some real estate. God will always multiply the fishes and the loaves you dedicate to Him and they will be able to feed the "five thousand," and more. If you give Him nothing to multiply you still have nothing. Life is not made up of all mountain-top experiences; therefore, not allowing for contingencies in the family budget is like going into business and not allowing for the hidden costs. No wonder that 80 percent or more of all the new businesses fail in one or two years. The family business must also be planned on a sound base, providing for the hidden costs. Jesus said,

> For which of you, intending to build a tower [high rise], sitteth not down first, and counteth the cost, whether he have sufficient to finish it? Lest haply, after he hath laid the foundation, and is not able to finish it, all that behold it begin to mock him. (Luke 14:28, 29)

Many couples, after years of married life, have very little idea what they would do if, for some unknown reason, they would not receive a pay check for only sixty days.

Unsuspected disruption of income often forces use of short-term, high-interest loans which can, in fact, put a continuing burden on the household, creating a grave crisis and resulting in a continuing struggle, disappointment, and frustration.

When we refer to percentages—in case your school math has gotten a bit rusty—let us give you a rule and an example. You always divide the smaller number by the larger number, adding a decimal and two zeros to find the percent:

$$\begin{array}{r} .20 \\ \$900 \overline{)\$180.00} \end{array} \quad \begin{array}{l} \text{The answer is 20\%} \\ \text{House payment} \end{array}$$

To prove your math, simply reverse the process and multiply. Then replace the position of the decimal:

$$.20 \times 900 = \$180.00$$

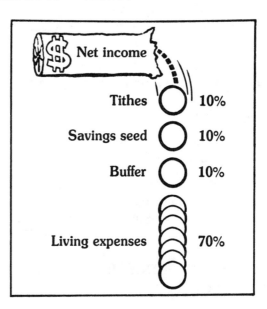

THE
10-10-10-70
PLAN

Net income

Tithes 10%

Savings seed 10%

Buffer 10%

Living expenses 70%

SAMPLE OF A FAMILY BUDGET SETUP
BUDGET FOR JOHN AND MARY DOE
AND FAMILY FOR JUNE, 1978:

I.   GROSS INCOME $_____

A. Payroll Taxes and
   Income Taxes $_____

B. Union Dues $_____

C. Tithes, 10% $_____

D. Other $_____

   Total Fixed Expenses
   (Lines A-D) $_____   -$_____

II.   GROSS WORKING INCOME $_____

A. Contingencies $_____

B. Savings (10% working
   income)—Seed money $_____

C. Buffer and Debts (20% percent
   of working income) $_____
                 Subtotal $_____ $_____
                                                  -$_____

**III.   NET SPENDABLE
       INCOME** $_____

Family Budget

IV. NET LIVING INCOME $_____

	Monthly Budgeted	Actual Expenses
A. Offerings	$_____	$_____
B. Rent or Mortgage	$_____	$_____
C. Utilities	$_____	$_____
D. Phone	$_____	$_____
E. Gasoline	$_____	$_____
F. Auto Maintenance	$_____	$_____
G. Auto Insurance	$_____	$_____
H. Other Insurance	$_____	$_____
I. Doctor and Medical	$_____	$_____
J. Food and Household	$_____	$_____
K. Clothes	$_____	$_____
L. Home Furnishings	$_____	$_____
M. Vacation	$_____	$_____
N. Allowances	$_____	$_____
O. Gifts and Benevolence	$_____	$_____
P. Recreation and Entertainment	$_____	$_____
Q. Other	$_____	$_____
R. _____	$_____	$_____
S. _____	$_____	$_____

Total—Budgeted and Actual $_____ $_____

Some of the items, such as recreation and entertainment, may surprise you. You may ask, "Do I budget for activities like this?" Some recreation is necessary for a happy life. Budget for it and set a goal. This way you and your spouse can have a night out. Plan and live for it all week long. Plan simple activities and life will not get monotonous. Get a baby-sitter and go out to eat or visit a home prayer group or attend a Full Gospel Business Men's dinner, or attend a gospel crusade. Remember, when you do things together, you will stay together. The little things you do will be remembered far longer than over-priced celebrations.

I still remember when, during the days following the Depression, my wife and I went out one evening a week. We would take the San Francisco Muni and for just five cents each we rode all over the city, all the way to the Ferry Building, again transferring to the cable car and up California Street to Fisherman's Wharf. All this ride for less than thirty cents for both of us.

We still remember the nickel hamburgers and how we joked with the waiter or fry cook. We asked him to tell us where he hid the meat. Good attitudes purchase more joy and happiness than can be purchased with the total assets of the Chase Manhattan Bank.

You will notice the 20 percent buffer in the budget is designated for emergencies and debts. This is in case you now have some debts, such as time payments, so you can deal with these culprits. These are referred to in the Scripture: "The borrower is servant to the lender" (Prov. 22:7).

One way of demonstrating the extent of this servitude is to multiply the amount of an average auto payment times the total months you have to pay and you may find that often a

Datsun may end up costing more on time than a Cadillac for cash. As soon as your family gets out of debt the whole additional 10 percent can be added to seed money.

In 1940 we lived in San Francisco and we noticed several of the young families who attended Glad Tidings Temple were buying new Chevrolets. Upon investigation we found these cars were selling for about $1,800. The salesman told us how we could buy a brand new Chevrolet on a thirty-six-month payment plan. When we got home and multiplied the monthly payment times thirty-six and added our down payment this increased the cost of the car to more than $2,400! That was $600 extra. We just were not willing to pay the additional interest; therefore, I began to look for an alternate method of buying the car we wanted. After about nine months of patient waiting some of the same model cars were beginning to show up on the used car lots. I found one with only 12,000 miles selling for $800, and it was as clean as a pin. In fact, the engine was just broken-in and the bugs had all been worked out. It ran like a top. My friends not only paid three times as much as I did for the same car, but also paid the new car insurance and license costs. This experience began to show me something new, demonstrating that the Scripture can become alive as a guide. The wisdom of God surpasses all the wisdom of the most learned economist.

> If any of you lack wisdom, let him ask of God, that giveth to all men liberally. (James 1:5)

Notice the words, "to all." This is a promise to anyone who asks, regardless of his I.Q., scholastic achievement, or training. There are no qualifications attached to God's promises except believing and obeying.

Include your children in your budget. Let them earn their allowance by participating in home chores. Allow them to learn financial responsibility and as soon as they begin to earn outside money, have them share some portion of family living costs. A Scripture that is often quoted and perhaps misapplied is: "Train up a child in the way he should go: and when he is old, he will not depart from it" (Prov. 22:6). But you seldom hear the following verse: "The rich ruleth over the poor and the borrower is servant to the lender" (Prov. 22:7).

These verses were not divided when originally written; they were in one paragraph. This Scripture may involve training children in financial responsibility so they will not become servants to the lenders.

You would be amazed at the satisfaction a child will gain if he is required to pay something to the mother for room and board, especially when he hears his father pray at the dinner table, "I thank you Lord for this meal which you have allowed my son or daughter to earn and provide, that we might have strength for our bodies. Bless him as he now is growing up to help us carry the burden of supplying the needs of this home. Amen."

Wow! What a reward! It is greater than that dirt bike or the skis which he bought from the rest of his earnings. Young people will appreciate clothes more when they pay for them.

During the Second World War, it was my lot to sail the Pacific Ocean with the merchant marine. This was the time of the Rome, Tokyo, Berlin Axis led by the three leaders: Mussolini, Tojo, and Hitler. They were opposed by the British, Chinese, Americans, and other nations. This was the most devastating world conflict since the time of Adam. The merchant ships were carrying supplies to the armed forces and were hunted by the Japanese submarines on the high seas. If found, merchant ships were sunk to prevent the supplies from reaching their destination. Each night we would have to sail without any external lights showing. The portholes were painted black to prevent light from escaping. The external bulkheads contained a set of double doors. The first door had to be closed before the second could be opened in order to trap the light. There was a watchman on the deck at all times, inspecting the ship for light which might be seen by an enemy submarine.

We often would travel a zigzag course to confuse the enemy, using the compass for direction and the clock for time. The course and time data was recorded on a chart. The deck officer would go out on the deck with a sextant (an instrument which looks similar to a surveyor's transit), and would take readings using certain stars, the sun or the moon in relation to the horizon, and the angles between them to verify our location and progress.

Similarly, a family using a budget must keep good records of expenditures in the categories listed in their budget to determine where they have been, where they are, and also to foresee the direction they are taking. This allows needed corrections in direction to be made.

During World War II it was important for us to know where we were and where we were headed, because many floating minefields had been planted by the Japanese and the Americans. Often the course had to be carefully steered through narrow corridors between these minefields. Otherwise, we would surely hit one of them. These mines were so powerful that one of them could sink the largest ship.

First, a family needs to work out a written budget. Secondly, they must have the motivation to use it, to stay on the proper course. The enemy of the family has planted many minefields. The dangers can be recognized in high interest rates, easy payment plans (what a misnomer!), and the impulsive lures of something-for-nothing gimmicks. All are like floating mines.

Carelessness not only can, but surely will, sink you. Satan confuses the Christian family in their finances. He knows exactly how to plant his mines to attack the family and rob them of joy, peace, and God's provisions.

Be sober, be vigilant; because your adversary the devil, as a roaring lion, walketh about, seeking whom he may devour. (1 Pet. 5:8)

May we suggest that you go to a stationery store and pick up two little pocket expense record books that give you a space for every day in the year. Some appointment books can also be utilized for these records and these are often given away free at many banks. Give one to your spouse and then both of you can write down everything you spend. With these two books and your checkbook record you can reconstruct everything in just a few minutes each month.

A word of caution. These records are not to be used as a weapon by each spouse to keep the other in line. Remember, if one partner does a good job in controlling spending, perhaps it will be a challenge to the other to do even better.

It is interesting that if one apologizes for some dumb expenditure the other mate will generally admit how they also had goofed and then together make the course correction, keeping the family ship of finance not only sailing safely but also delivering its cargo to your family and having resources left over to spread the gospel. Putting seed plan and budgeting to work in your family will increase the value of the income to contribute to your church, missionaries, charities, or other worthy ministries the Lord would lead you to support.

Some time ago, I was sharing with a friend, Mr. Joseph Yang, a brilliant economist, who represented the Chinese government when the United Nations Charter was established in San Francisco after the Second World War. I consider Mr. Yang to be one of our nation's most brilliant economists and a wonderful Christian man. On one occasion, he and I were counseling some new Christians who were having a difficult time steering a successful financial course for their families. In the process Joe and I compared the way we budget for our families and we found similarities in that neither of us had any monthly payments to make. As a result we each gave more toward spreading the gospel than we were using for our families, even though we were living very well. Out of that conversation came some helpful suggestions:

1. Deposit all your income in a checking account. This will make record keeping much easier.

2. Write a check for all major items, including one to yourself for petty cash and allowances.

3. Keep a check and distribution record. It will help you to analyze how your income is spent.

4. Keep one good record up-to-date, for God supplies all of your income and if you are faithful in a few things, He will bless you in many.

5. Each month prepare a monthly budget to keep inside your checkbook as a convenient reminder.

6. Remember, the purpose of saving is not that you may have money to buy what you want or what you think you need. The goal is that money would work for you, giving you not only prosperity but income in those years when you will no longer be employed.

Interest Payments

Interest payments are culprits. They have the most profound effects, eating deeply into the family budget. These culprits eat at the future, both financial and spiritual—reducing your sense of well-being. These interest culprits also have a definite dampening effect on your prayers and relationship with God. Eternal life really begins here on earth. Therefore, eliminate everything that reduces communion with Jesus now so that close communion can be assured in heaven.

Every family should strive as quickly as possible to eliminate all interest payments by making all purchases with cash, except real estate. "The borrower is servant to the lender" (Prov. 22:7).

Let's review a promise, "The Lord shall open unto thee his good treasure, the heaven to give the rain unto thy land in his season, and to bless all the work of thine hand: and thou shalt lend unto many nations, and thou shalt not borrow" (Deut. 28:12). Why didn't God want His children to borrow? It was simple; borrowing would make them slaves. This may be difficult for you to do at first; however, if your children are grown you may be able to sell the large house and buy a smaller one for cash, so that there will be no interest payments. No one has ever been able to show me anything he has bought with his interest payments. Interest dollars fall into a pit from which they can never be retrieved. Young families without much cash should follow a conservative pattern and not buy a larger house than they actually need. Review your *needs* apart from your *wants*. Plan to have funds available for the costs of college or Bible school as soon as your children finish high school. Most children crave and want love far more than the plush house or even their own car.

In our own case, we lived in a 1400-square-foot house during the time our three children were teen-agers. Some of our friends with families the same size as ours were buying 2,000 and 3,000-square-feet homes and were making monthly payments of $400 to $600 a month.

More than ten years have passed since then. Let us look at the results. None of our children have ever hit the drug scene nor turned their backs on us. We are proud of all of our children. In fact, I am always excited when visiting our children and grandchildren and to be able to attend their church and Sunday school with them. Our son, who has not married yet, was instrumental in bringing his Jewish buddy to the saving knowledge of Christ.

Now let us look at some of our friends, who overspent, requiring both the husband and wife to work full-time, leaving the children to almost raise themselves. Several of their children have turned to drugs and, without a miracle from God, are lost to the kingdom. Some are separated and divorced and many have even left the faith and now live in a state away from God.

Some time back, a couple named John and Helen came to

me for counseling. This couple just did not understand the effects of credit on their family finances. Their pattern was to buy their two cars, clothing, gasoline, camera, luggage, and airline tickets all on time payments. And, as frequently happens, they would have to refinance their debts periodically. They were playing a game of credit roulette.

In Russian roulette the player puts one cartridge in the revolver and spins its cylinder. Then he puts the gun to his head and pulls the trigger. The odds are five to one that he will not lose, for there are six slots in a revolver. For those who lose, it is suicide. In credit roulette there are even fewer chances of winning because every additional purchase puts another bullet into the gun. If you continue, you soon will be the victim of financial suicide.

The habit of charging by just signing a contract to pay high interest often leads to having too many bills for the income available. Then, often, a consolidation loan is required with interest rates from 20 to 30 percent or even more. These victims are now hooked on credit and there can be no freedom until they are willing to take the cure.

John and Helen had no idea what buying on credit really cost them nor how clever the designers of credit sales were and how they are armed with the most sophisticated computerized sales schemes. The credit industry knows the average family income in any city, and how much can be siphoned off by selling products on time payments.

Many good and unsuspecting couples are financially safer in a dark alley in one of our large cities than in the most brilliantly lighted department stores, or the new car and boat shows.

The United States government requires the manufacturer

to put warning signs on many harmful products, to protect the unsuspecting purchaser. In the same fashion, the government requires warning signs to be put on credit purchases with the "Truth in Lending Laws." If you read this information, telling what harm it can do to your family budget, undoubtedly you will say, "No thank you!"

Dr. Robert Hicks of the American Institute of Family Relations states, "I have never counseled with a couple who are having difficulties in marriage where they operated on a budget."

There are more than one thousand passages in the Bible that give wisdom in handling money and material possessions. Sixteen of the thirty-eight parables of Christ also deal with money and earthly possessions.

The family budget is like a road map, telling your dollars where to go. Without it you wonder where they went. Anyone with an uncontrollable desire do buy things can very easily find financial salvation in a budget if he is willing to follow and use it faithfully.

The purpose of a family budget is to balance your outgo with your income.

Some families I know use the following guidelines in planning their family budget:

1. Your shelter should not exceed 20 percent of your net income.

2. Transportation, auto maintenance, and gas should not exceed 10 percent of net income.

3. Food and household expenses should not exceed 20 percent. Many families waste a lot of money in the grocery store because purchases are not based on nutrition and food value. Food merchants are experts in using hidden

persuaders; they know that the average shopper in a supermarket buys 30 percent more than he needs. Brightly colored cartons have a greater effect on sales than the quality of the product inside of them. It has been proven many times. The average housewife will buy items on easily reached shelves even though better buys may be on a higher or lower shelf. Shopping carts are designed so they can be filled without much effort. This induces extensive buying.

In his book, *The Hidden Persuaders*, Vance Packard refers to studies made by the duPont Company and the Folding Paper Box Association. These studies show that about two-thirds of all purchases in the supermarket are completely or partially influenced by impulse. The *Progressive Grocer* puts the figure at about the same fraction.

James Vicary, a motivational analyst, used partially hidden cameras to record the behavior pattern of shoppers from the time they entered a supermarket, through all their shopping, and up to the check-out counter. The results were startling, even to Vicary. The experiment was based on the fact that the rate a person blinks his eyes reflects his state of inner tension. The average person, according to Mr. Vicary, normally blinks about thirty-two times a minute. As the individual's state of tension increases, he will blink more frequently. Extensive tension will produce up to sixty blinks a minute. When noticeably relaxed, on the other hand, the eye blink rate may drop to a subnormal twenty times a minute or less.

It was noted that as a shopper enters the display area, the eye blink rate, instead of going up to indicate mounting tension, goes down and down and down to the very low rate of fourteen blinks per minute. The shopper falls into a state much like a light hypnotic trance. One reason for this, Mr.

Vicary observed, is that the supermarket of today is packed with products that only kings and queens could afford in former years.

Interestingly, the shoppers were observed to be in such a trance that they passed by neighbors and friends without even noticing or greeting them. They would wander about the store in a glassy stare, plucking things at random and bumping into boxes without seeing them. They did not notice the camera clicking away, often within one-and-a-half feet from their faces. Vicary also noticed that when the shoppers had filled their carts (or satisfied themselves) and started toward the check-out counter, their eye blink count rose to twenty-five blinks per minute. Then, at the sound of the cash register bell and the voice of the clerk asking for money, the eye blink rate rose again to exceed the normal to forty-five blinks per minute. In many cases it turned out that the shoppers did not have enough money to pay for all the nice things they had put in their carts.

The 60,000,000 American shoppers who go to the supermarkets each week are getting "help" in their purchases and "splurchases" from motivational psychologists and psychiatrists who are hired by the food merchandisers.

On May 18, 1956, *The New York Times* printed a remarkable interview with a young man named Gerald Stahl, the vice president of the Packaging Designers' Council. He stated: "Psychologists say that people have so much to choose from that they want help. They would like the package that hypnotizes them into picking it." He urges food packers to put more hypnosis into their package designing so that the package will act as a flashlight waved in front of the customer's eyes. Often, shoppers will pick the hypnotic package instead of a rival.

Mr. Stahl found that it takes an average shopper approximately twenty seconds to cover a supermarket aisle. According to the supermarket industry's philosophy, the shopper should not be able to read the package while it is on the shelf but only when it is picked up. Very seldom, after being picked up, will it be put back on the shelf.

When the shopper is buying without a definite shopping list, the merchandising studies show that at least 30 percent more is purchased than when one shops with one. Therefore, 30 percent is spent unnecessarily. Often very little thought is given to the nourishment needs of the family. A lot of junk food is made of highly refined products including sugar, white flour, and food preservatives that contribute to malnutrition and sickness.

Apparently the ones most prone to splurge when they get into the supermarket are husbands and children. Supermarket operators pretty well agree that husbands are easy marks for all sorts of impulse items and cite cases where the husband was sent to the store for a loaf of bread and departs with both of his arms loaded with his favorite snack items.

Some supermarket operators put dozens of little carts in their stores which small children can push about. People think children are cute as they go zipping around the store, imitating mom. They grab boxes of cookies, candy, dog and cat food and whatever delights or interests them. Complications arise when mother and child come out of the trance at the check-out counter. The store operator gleefully relates what often happens: "There is usually a wrangle when the mother sees what her child has put into his basket. She tries to make him take the items back. This usually causes him to bawl and kick before he will surrender the cookies, candy, Popsicles, and soft drinks, so they usually stay for the family."

If this pattern is true in supermarket buying, what about large items like a car or a home?

There was a study made in New London, Connecticut, showing that shoppers are lethargic and casual even when making the most important purchase they'll make in a decade—the purchase of a home.

Half the people looking for homes who were studied looked at less than six before they made their selection. Nineteen percent looked at two houses before buying and 10 percent looked at only one.

Saving has been overlooked by most Americans. One estimate I recently saw stated that only 7 percent of the nation's wage earners save or invest any part of their salary. For the most part, people save to be able to spend. Therefore, they are really saving nothing.

Wealth is not based on money you work for, but on money that works for you.

Understanding this principal makes the difference. A rule for financial success is to keep part of every dollar you earn and put it to work for you. Thereby, you become your own best creditor. If you wait to save from what you have left over, there will never be any. So pay your tithes; second, deposit your savings. This pattern is of prime importance. Savings for investment and multiplication will bring financial success and freedom.

Many people who live their lives concerned about nothing

more than news, weather, T.V., food, shelter, raiment, and entertainment are not using their full potentials for God.

8

WHAT IS A
GOOD INVESTMENT?

WHOSE ADVICE SHOULD I LISTEN TO?

There are so many so-called "experts."

I am reminded of a German family who, in 1953, built a fifty-unit apartment house in Livermore, California. The father was in his late sixties and he was always puttering around the project. His three sons, in their thirties and early forties were busily helping him build the project. The father said to me, "This is my third project—one for each boy." Not being the best-skilled carpenters, the boys did the rough construction and then hired finishers to complete the building. I remember how the building was swarming with various tradesmen. There were electricians, plumbers, plasterers, tile layers, and cement finishers. The father would always take the left-over plaster or cement at the end of the day and make a waterfall with a miniature mountain and fountains. One day a plasterer came and said to the man, "You are doing this all wrong," even though the father was having the time of his life. I remember how he looked up at the plasterer, with a twinkle in his eye, and said, "You tell me that I do not know what I do? Vell, I tell to you. How much you worth? I worth more than a million. I do not think I listen to you."

There are a lot of people who are always ready to give advice, but a good rule is to look first at their successes before you listen to their advice. The Bible says, "By their fruits ye shall know [understand] them" (Matt. 7:20).

There is also an old saying which I am sure you have heard many times, "The proof is in the pudding." This can be applied here, where theories have little weight when they are compared to facts.

Many successful men and women are willing to freely share their experiences with you if you only ask them to. "Freely ye have received, freely give" (Matt. 10:8).

Run away as fast as you can from get-rich-quick schemes. Emotional sales pitches, the hunting lodge, the upholstery shop, the little restaurant, the commercial fishing boat are all one's dreams but they are limited to time and energy. This is unlike the income from real estate, compounding interest, church notes, or tax-free public bonds.

Let us look at some of the items that have a sound basis.

INCOME REAL ESTATE AND ITS POTENTIAL

Income real estate has made more people rich in America than any other commodity, profession, or trade. One former employee of the telephone company began with $1000 invested in a house which he refinished and traded for multiples within a year. He tells fantastic stories of how he was able to pyramid this initial one thousand dollar investment to three million dollars in twenty years and retire with an income far in excess of his needs.

You may ask, "Is this an isolated case?" No, not at all. Who do you think owns all the apartment houses and commercial and industrial buildings in your town? Is it the big corporations? Not generally. These buildings, even though they are occupied by the big corporations are generally owned by many people you rub shoulders with daily. They have learned the law of harvest and disciplined themselves to save a portion of their income and invest it instead of trying to satisfy an insatiable appetite to spend every dime they have. This type of spender will always have financial problems, for it is so difficult for God to bless them by multiplying what they have. Remember, when you multiply nothing by one million, you still have a million nothings.

WHAT IS A GOOD BUY?

In looking for a good buy we must realize nothing is a good buy without good management. You have heard it is luck that makes money for people. That is a fallacy. Christians must discipline their lives to grow spiritually, and they also must discipline their financial lives to be able to prosper.

Christ often talked about good management of property and the bad results of poor management.

To get a 10 percent return on your investment, you need to

follow the following formula:

EXAMPLE: Triplex
Total Annual Income: $900 Month x 12 = $10,800
Taxes Based on Purchase
    Price: - 3,500
Insurance: - 900
Utilities and Services: - 300
    Net Annual Income: $6,100
The market value of this property is:
                              $6,100 x 10 = $61,000

I would like to warn you that there are all kinds of sales gimmicks relating to cash flow that do not usually have a solid foundation. So do not be deceived. Remember, the cash flow gives you no return on the money you spend on the down payment. Understand the difference between yield and cash flow.

After purchasing the income rental property, make a point to become a friend to your tenants. It not only pays dividends but it also permits Christian witnessing. You do not have to sacrifice firm and good collection policies. In fact, if you are lax in this area you will not be respected.

Any increase in income on your property will raise its market value. A landlord in Southern California supplied twenty-four garbage cans for his apartment house. One morning before the garbage was to be picked up he went and compacted all the garbage with his foot. In the process he found out that each can was only two-thirds full. So the next week he removed eight cans, leaving only sixteen. The savings amounted to $3.00 per month per can or $288 per year, which in turn resulted in $288 more net profit at the end of the year. So the value of the property is based on the net annual income. When he went to sell the apartment house, he was able to ask $2,880 more because he removed eight garbage cans. If you are a good manager of what God has entrusted you with, you will have a lot of fun and will have many good conversations between you, God, and your fellow man.

Lastly, you may ask, "Why is income real estate generally a good investment when properly managed?"

There is one principal reason: *While the tenants indirectly are paying off the mortgage the property is becoming yours.*

You may feel you are not capable of being a good manager and that may be true; however, good managers are not *born*, they are *made*. Good stewards of God's blessings are not born; they are made. A sincere effort on our part will do wonders. I suggest that you set a realistic goal like saving 10 percent of your income. Put it in a savings account until you get a thousand dollars or so. Then increase the interest rate with a time certificate, perhaps at the same bank for a year while you save another thousand or two. Set a goal of $5000 in two or three years. At that point you may be ready to look at income property such as a duplex.

Here are some guidelines which are almost foolproof. You should always require a minimum of 10 percent return on your investment. The real estate agents will tell you that it is not available. Don't you believe it! They may be hard to find at times, but keep looking; before long one will show up.

The Type of Real Estate You Should Not Buy

The vacant land that you think will become more valuable with years and has every indication to do so may be nothing but a trap which will siphon all your savings. This has happened to millions of people, especially since taxes and interest are becoming so high. The salesmen will have such glowing reports; in fact they will often provide a dinner, or a plane trip to some remote place where they want to sell you a five-acre ranchette. When you get there you may see portions of a street and a few houses. Everything may look positive. Thousands of people have invested their life's savings in this type of land only to find when the salesman sold enough land to make a bundle, he withdrew the money out of the development company as wages. The company then went bankrupt, leaving thousands of stranded people with literally useless land.

There are thousands of people who have heard how someone made big money by buying a parcel of land in the path of growth near a city as the land developed around them. For each one who has made money this way, *literally dozens have not.*

I personally learned of a firm from Connecticut that heard land in California was a good buy. As a result, they purchased at least two hundred acres or more in the town of Livermore for about $800,000. At the time, the city was doubling in size every five years, and they did not think they had a chance of losing.

The concern for clean air took place nationwide and concerned Livermore citizens also organized a political momentum headed by a brilliant and aggressive physicist. This man was elected to the city council and even became the mayor. When appointment to the planning commission and other committees were made, the political machine headed by him brought sympathizers who swamped the council as volunteers, many with high scholastic abilities and qualifications. There were wives of PhD's, men with master's degrees—all eager to save the environment. It soon became evident that the environment they had captured was the control of the planning commission and, as a result, growth in Livermore began to grind to a halt. The environmentalists' next move was to stop the previously-approved expansion of the sewer plant, even though the state and federal governments were paying for 87½ percent of the construction costs.

The next move was to get an initiative on the local ballot restricting the issuance of building permits because there was not enough capacity at the sewer plant.

A strong campaign pointed to the health dangers if growth were allowed to proceed, and this stop-growth initiative passed at the ballot box. The unconstitutionality of the initiative was contested in local and state courts and millions of dollars worth of time and legal fees were supplied by the taxpayers to settle the issue. In the meantime, growth almost stopped; my friends from Connecticut were sitting with a million dollars of prime Livermore land without a market in the foreseeable future, paying over $40,000 in property taxes annually plus losing at least $100,000 in interest each year.

This can be summarized in one sentence. *Don't buy bare land unless you are going to build on it that very year and have the permit to build in your hand before you buy it!* Bare land can be compared to an alligator; the more you feed it the bigger its appetite becomes. Every time you see a parcel of vacant land someone is showing you, visualize this alligator that is eager to eat you out of your present house which is your home.

Why income real estate is generally a good investment:

1. The value of real estate has increased since the Indians sold Manhattan island and Russia sold Alaska except for a short period during the Depression years in the late 1920s.
2. Income property can provide for a tax shelter which is very important to your financial growth, and income property provides capital gains.

CHURCH NOTES OR BONDS

Church bonds have been perhaps the safest form of investment known due to the stringent regulations by the state and federal governments, especially in the small, growing churches. The ones which are sold with compounded interest will amaze you. For instance, I bought a $250 bond for each of my grandchildren in August of 1976 at 9 percent compounded interest. In February of 1995 each young adult will get $1,343. This is almost five and a half times what I put in; at the same time I saved the church money because the bank wanted 11% percent interest plus a substantial fee known as points.

You will find that when the interest is compounded at 9 percent every eight years the original sum doubles. Let's assume when your son is 20, instead of buying him that $5,000 car, you decided to buy him a 9 percent church bond.

What Is a Good Investment?

Here is how that seed money will grow:

20 years old	$ 5,000
28 years old	10,000
36 years old	20,000
44 years old	40,000
52 years old	80,000
60 years old	160,000
65 years old	260,000

This is just plain mathematics and just imagine how easy for you to be enslaved when you are paying the interest and the process is in reverse.

OTHER INVESTMENTS.

There are many types of investments such as:

A. Individual Retirement Accounts.
B. Banks.
C. Mutual Funds.
D. Savings and Loans.
E. Mortgages.
F. Common Stock.
G. Limited Partnerships.
H. Government Bonds.
I. Christian Organizations and Businesses.

The investments just listed generally do not generate the rapid growth that good income real estate does but, on the other hand, they often require less personal attention. One example can be cited that a person who will save twenty dollars per week in a regular savings account paying 5¼ percent per annum will have an investment that will grow to $70,925 at the end of thirty years. If he had a planned investment at 8 percent per annum, his investment would

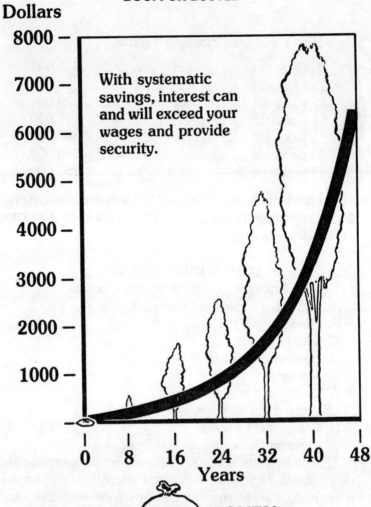

Dollars

With systematic savings, interest can and will exceed your wages and provide security.

Years

GROWTH OF (SEED) MONEY:

$100.00 compounded at 9% will double every eight years and in 48 years will grow to a total of $6400.00.

grow to $127,240.

I suggest that before choosing an investment you investigate the risk factor and collateral involved. These two terms can be defined as follows:

(1.) "Risk factor" represents the chance there is that you may lose some or all of your investment.
(2.) "Collateral" is the value of the item you may sell if the borrower doesn't make the payments that he has promised.

You may wonder why we did not include insurance as an investment. Insurance fills a specific need, providing a protection to the family when the children are young. I recommend the purchase of term insurance and get the protection you feel necessary. Whole life insurance includes a savings plan and costs four or five times as much as term insurance for the equal amount of coverage. The interest earnings on the whole life policy are very low, approximately 2¼ to 3½ percent per annum. You are paying for two things in whole life insurance, protection and savings. Insurance policies that give dividends cost even more than whole life policies. In fact, the United States treasury decision number 1743 has declared the "dividend" as a return of overcharged premiums. What we are really saying is that insurance is a very poor form of savings or investment.

Do not co-sign notes.
   Six different passages say something about being a co-signer on a note. This should make you sit up and take notice. These Scriptures are: Proverbs 6:1-5, 11:15, 17:18,

20:16, 22:26-29, and 27:13. Look especially at: "If thou hast nothing to pay, why should he take away thy bed from under thee?" (Prov. 22:27).

The Bible, in fact, teaches if you are already in the position of co-signer, you should go to the individual, get down on your hands and knees, and beg him to let you out of the obligation.

Why is it wrong? First, it generally destroys relationships and friendships. People who generally need co-signers have difficulty managing their finances. They are not likely to change and your co-signing makes it possible for them to continue in their financial mismanagement. Secondly, a co-signer assumes a different position than one who guarantees. In fact, legally, he assumes the liability, even before the principal borrower defaults.

I have been asked, "Should I co-sign for my son and daughter, as they are only getting started? If not, how are they going to be able to buy a car or other items on credit?"

My response is, "First, stop and think through what you are saying to them by your actions. Are you telling them that God is not sufficient to meet their needs, but that you are the one they must look to to buy the first car, furniture, or lease an apartment?"

The Scripture plainly says that one should not enter this relationship even as a parent because it destroys faith and puts your children under bondage to the lender. May I offer an approach that involves trusting God and standing on His Word?

But my God shall supply all your need according to his riches in glory by Christ Jesus. (Phil. 4:19)

YOU CAN TAKE IT OFF YOUR INCOME TAX.

This is a statement often made by people who believe this is possible. They think they can deduct interest, medical expenses, and certain travel actually from their income tax. They remind me of Bud, an electrical supply salesman, who in 1952 used to sell me wire and electrical devices. Bud was an outgoing person and a pleasure to be with. One spring morning he came roaring into my driveway in a brand new shining red Oldsmobile Sports Coupe with the top down. Bud's voice boomed out, "Ed, let's go for a ride!"

We did this, and we also tried out all the new features such as power brakes, dual horns, and even the acceleration and road handling. Bud told me he paid $3,800 for the Olds instead of $2,100 for a two-door Ford many other salesmen were buying. Then he began to tell me how he was going to make money by having the more expensive car because he could take more money off his income tax. I smiled and congratulated him on his wisdom and suggested that he should buy four more Oldsmobiles; perhaps he could save so much money that he could quit working all together. He soon realized how foolish his reasoning was because the only real effect it had was to reduce his gross income.

Remember, you must first make the money, then any tax exempt expenditure only reduces your income. Tax is not an income and cannot be spent on anything. A leech never feeds a cow; the cow always is the one which feeds the leech.

To get set free, "Owe no man any thing, but to love one another" (Rom 13:8). You ask if it's wrong to buy a car on time? Wrong is not so because someone tells you it is wrong. Wrong is wrong because if you do wrong there will be a consequence you will have to pay and this fact is supported by God's Word. To have disbelief is wrong not because of a negative or positive act but it separates you from fellowship with God and that is what makes disbelief wrong. To buy on time is not wrong because you buy but because it enslaves you, thereby destroying your ability to save seed money where God can bless its growth.

No Seed = No Crop
No Savings = No Prosperity

IS IT WRONG TO BUY INCOME REAL ESTATE ON TIME PAYMENTS?

One day a lady asked me, "Is it wrong to buy income property on time?"

My answer was, "No, because income property appreciates; it does not depreciate like other goods."

She asked another question, "Does not the Scripture say, 'Owe no man anything'?"

"Yes, it does. But really you don't owe the mortgage holder anything because he has more than 100 percent security and the property continues to increase in value. This differs from other merchandise which loses value with time. Further, your tenants, by paying rent, are indirectly making the payments on principal, interest, taxes, and insurance. Your equity grows and your seed compounds and multiplies over and over again."

Credit-card buying often produces a debt without any security. Suppose you pay for a hotel lodging, gasoline which is used, food which is eaten, or clothing which becomes worn; where is the security to the lender? In fact, generally there is none; therefore, this type of lender charges the highest interest rates.

This type of buying can be compared to the biblical story of two brothers. One was hungry and the other had a bowl of beans. In their bargaining, the bowl of beans was purchased with the other's birthright. As a result of Esau's foolish credit buying, he was forced to continue to pay—for the remainder of his life (Gen. 25:27-34).

9

THE MOST PRECIOUS
COMMODITY YOU HAVE

Time is the most valuable commodity given to man by God, and yet no doubt you have heard many say, "It didn't cost me anything but my time." Therefore, the meaning is "I really got it for nothing."

In response I usually ask, "Did you? Or did it cost you a portion of the most precious commodity you have?"

Because time is generally a scarce commodity, and we all have just one lifetime's worth, we need to budget our time carefully. This should not be pressured, however, for that causes tension which results in inefficiency.

Time demands action. Even idle time, which goes beyond

the point of relaxing, calls for keeping busy with jigsaw puzzles, hobbies, etc. The Scripture says, "Where there is no vision the people perish" (Prov. 29:18). In many cases, idle people die and do not continue to live fulfilling lives whereas busy people tend to live longer.

Virgil, a good friend of mine who soon will retire at the age of sixty-five from the Lawrence Laboratory, shared with me one day about the survival rate of laboratory retirees. Their statistics show that a man retiring from that facility at sixty-five lives on the average eighteen additional months without regard to his health at retirement. What happens I do not know for sure, but it certainly makes us take notice of *busy* people who continue into their eighties and even longer.

A few weeks ago Chuck, a city inspector, was telling me he was about to retire from his city job and move into the country. I shared with him what Virgil said about the retirees he knew, to interest him in considering a meaningful Christian ministry. He assured me he would be gardening and "doing the things he always wanted to do and did not have time for." Only four days later I received the news that Chuck had had a massive heart attack and was in the Valley Memorial Hospital.

I have a lot of difficulty with all the songs about our sorrows being over and this dreadful life being finished. I was fifty-four years old when I got set free in the Spirit and the good Lord and I have so much to do I seem to never get it done. The Lord fills one day after another with a new story to tell those with whom I come in contact.

Several weeks ago a group of men and women had an all-day worship and praise meeting in Soledad Prison. There were twelve Spirit-filled, Christian people of all faiths in our group. There were Catholics, Pentecostals, Methodists, and a Jew by the name of Al Boucher. Some of the group were singing, some were praising God as we walked through the yard toward the front gate. I asked Al Boucher, who is a volunteer chaplain, "Where is Juan Corona's cell?" Juan was allegedly convicted of killing over twenty Mexican migrant workers in the Yuba City area several years ago and burying their bodies under peach trees in shallow graves.

Pointing to a cell block, Al replied, "The third window from the end. That is the lock-up area."

I asked, "What kind of a man is Juan?"

"Oh, he is a terrible man. He will not listen to you and when I tried to talk to him, you know what his reply was to me? He said, 'I would like to bury *you* under a peach tree.'"

My reply to Al was, "Does not the Scripture say that whosoever will may come to Jesus—even the vilest sinners He was willing to save?" As we continued to walk I began to pray out loud for Juan Corona with a sensation of belief that God would do this. The following Friday a men's retreat was held in the Santa Cruz Mountains. We arrived just before dark and as we drove into these beautiful grounds, surrounded by the big California redwoods, with the wonderful fresh smell that is only present in this type of forest, I saw Al Boucher running toward me calling out, "Guess what happened. Juan Corona gave his heart to Jesus."

I asked, "How did it happen? Was he in one of your services?"

He answered, "No, it was sometime during the night while he was alone in his cell."

Truly, I was excited because here, I, a nothing, was prompted by God to pray for a man I presumed to be the world's cruelest sinner. Then I learned God gave him a new heart.

Another point about killing time: I am looking forward to when time will be no longer measured, when Jesus and I can walk and talk together. I am suggesting a time budget, which will help you to adjust to the Holy Spirit who can direct your life.

TIME BUDGET

A WEEK CONSISTS OF 148 HOURS

1.	Worship alone with God	4 Hours
2.	Work	40 Hours
3.	Sleep	45 Hours
4.	Home and Family	
	A. Family Sharing Evening	4 Hours
	B. Meals	10 Hours
	C. House and Yard Work	14 Hours
	D. Recreation	4 Hours
	E. Shopping	2 Hours
5.	Night out with spouse	4 Hours
6.	*Christian Service*	
	A. Church	4 Hours
	B. Home Prayer Meeting	4 Hours
	C. Prison and Hospital Ministry	4 Hours
	D. Full Gospel Business Men's Meetings	3 Hours
7.	Management of Seed Money	6 Hours
		148 Hours

Give time to God's service and He will add to your income, joy, happiness, and give you a sense of success. He does not want you to make yourself godly because only He can do this for you.

It was not until I was willing to put God's Word on my office walls and Christian literature on the end tables and Scripture mottos on the walls and to share Jesus with everyone that my time became efficient. I have truly seen men bring me their land, which they could not sell, and ask me to make something of it. This year I had one man pay me $40,000 above what I had intended to ask for a piece of property. This was a nice payment for all the time I spent on the radio, prison ministry, men's luncheons and counseling. God is the greatest employer of all.

God always begins to bless you financially when you witness Christ to others. Prosperity was always coupled with obedience to God. You may ask, "What were God's instructions for us to obey?" In the words of Jesus, "Go ye into all the world, and preach the gospel to every creature" (Mark 16:15). Many of these creatures are found on your job, at the trade club, union meetings, or at the P.T.A.

10

GOD'S PROVISION
THROUGH YOUR JOB

"The steps of a good man are ordered by the Lord" (Ps. 37:23). Do you believe you work on a job God actually gave you and that the payroll check you receive is a direct provision from God? Or do you have a job that bugs you, and the people you work with literally drive you up the wall? Does it seem that everything your supervisor and co-workers do is done to make it rough on you until you hate to go to work and wouldn't if you had any other choice, but because of the wolf outside the door you continue to go, all the while really feeling trapped? There can be a great release in the Lord, who can change your supervisor completely around without his even knowing it, when you extend the gift of love toward your employer or supervisor.

During the fifteenth century many Christians were burned at the stake for their profession of Jesus Christ. A layer of straw was spread around their feet and pieces of wood were laid over the straw. Alternate layers of straw and wood were stacked until they reached the chin of the comdemned. After lighting the combination of straw and wood it burned so furiously that it quickly cremated the body. Some of the Christians, although tied to the stake, would have their arms free. With their free hands they would actually help the executioners with the straw and the wood as they placed it around their bodies and all the while they continued to speak to them about the wonderful love of Jesus. We are told that this act of love often melted the hard hearts of the executioners who later accepted Jesus as their Savior.

I heard an interesting story that inspired my faith. The laymen of a Baptist church in Stockton, California, agreed in 1955 to be thankful to God for their jobs, and they came up with the idea that because an eight-hour day had 480 minutes and 10 percent (tithe of time) was forty-eight minutes, they would give God the first forty-eight minutes of each working day. Because they were working for God during the first forty-eight minutes—from 8:00 A.M. to 8:48 A.M., they arrived at the job on time. They were efficient. They were pleasant, with songs of praise in their hearts. In fact, the whole place of employment became a place where they were very happy to be. What were the results?

Beaming with excitement, some were promoted to supervisors, some got raises, all of them received more satisfaction from their jobs. Some had such love for their bosses that with tears of love they prayed for the very supervisors they had hated just three months earlier.

"Servants, be obedient to them that are your masters according to the flesh, with fear and trembling, in singleness of your heart, as unto Christ; Not with eyeservice, as menpleasers; but as the servants of Christ, doing the will of God from the heart; With good will doing service, as to the Lord, and not to men: Knowing that whatsoever good thing any man doeth, the same shall he receive of the Lord, whether he be bond [slave] or free" (Eph. 6:5-8).

"Servants, obey in all things your masters according to the flesh; not with eyeservice, as menpleasers; but in singleness of heart fearing God: And whatsoever ye do, do it heartily, as to the Lord, and not unto men; Knowing that of the Lord ye shall receive the reward of the inheritance: for ye serve the Lord Christ. But he that doeth wrong shall receive for the wrong which he hath done: and there is no respect of persons" (Col. 3:22-25).

"Let as many servants as are under the yoke count their own masters worthy of all honour, that the name of God and his doctrine be not blasphemed" (1 Tim. 6:1).

"Servants, be subject to your masters with all fear; not only to the good and gentle, but also to the forward. For this is thankworthy, if a man for conscience toward God endure grief, suffering wrongfully. For what glory is it, if when ye be buffeted for your faults, ye shall take it patiently? but if, when ye do well, and suffer for it, ye take it patiently, this is acceptable with God" (1 Pet. 2:18-20).

If you feel that God is not using you on your job, review your attitudes.

BOOM OR BUSTED

In 1976 we were constructing a church school building. It is a two-story structure made of twenty concrete panels, twenty feet wide, twenty-seven feet high and each weighing twenty-seven tons. We had told the people of the church when these walls would be raised and many gathered to see this feat in construction. The crane we used had a tall boom raised more than one hundred feet into the air. About one hundred people gathered, and after prayer, the lifting operation began. The cables were hooked into the lifting eyes on the panel and, with a signal, the sixty-five-ton, giant crane lifted the first panel. The people cheered as it was set into place and the steel braces were attached to keep it in place. The cables were soon attached to the second panel and, as it began to tilt, it suddenly broke in half. This break was very serious and costly because the crane and rigging crew cost over $3,000 a day and they had to stop work until a new panel was poured.

My carpenter foreman was observing the crew and my reactions. Many of the crew were not Christians. Some began to curse. One threw his safety hat on the ground in anger; others threw their hammers. It was not their fault, for I had engineered the panels myself, and was hurt financially. I remember the calm God gave me and the wisdom to deal with the situation.

My carpenter foreman who had worked for me for four years gave his heart to Jesus a short time after this incident and is now a wonderful Christian. I wonder what would have happened if I had taken the attitude that the situation was so bad that it gave me the right to curse and rave. The $3,500 loss in this accident was a small price to pay for the opportunity and privilege of portraying the witness of Jesus in a crucial time on the job.

I wondered what would happen if you could see your boss as he or she is—actually the person God set over you so that His will could be perfected in and through you. You say, "How can this be, for my boss is a sinner and does many things in a way that I think is wrong?" Your suspicions may all be true, but until you learn the lessons God wants to teach you, He may not promote you.

"Knowing this, that the trying of your faith worketh patience. But let patience have her perfect work, that ye may be perfect and entire, wanting nothing" (James 1:3, 4).

I challenge you to look for the wonderful hand of God in your job, your boss, and your fellow workers. If you accept the challenge, the whole world will open up to you in a new way, and God's blessing will begin to roll into your life with joy in the Spirit which will overwhelm you.

"Never be lazy in your work but serve the Lord enthusiastically. Be glad for all God is planning for you. Be patient in trouble, and prayerful always. If someone mistreats you because you are a Christian, don't curse him; pray that God will bless him" (Rom. 12:11, 12, 14 TLB).

Remember, God is not only a source of power but He gives His children power to become successful. God is interested in your job, interested that you prosper, and interested in your bank account. "I am the Lord thy God which teacheth thee to profit, which leadeth thee by the way that thou shouldest go" (Isa. 48:17).

"In all thy ways acknowledge him, and he shall direct thy paths" (Prov. 3:6).

Many Christians are confused and think they are living in

When the accident took place, the unsaved cursed and were upset, but God gave me a calm allowing me to cope with the circumstances.

two worlds—a Christian world in church and a devil's world on the job. A release in the Holy Spirit will make a continual walk with God in both worlds possible and joyful. And then you will discover that there was really only one world all along.

Faithfulness to your employer is a very important ingredient necessary toward your financial prosperity. The faithful stewardship of time on your job is a direct reflection of your faithfulness to God. God said in His Word: "Work hard and become a leader; be lazy and never succeed" (Prov. 12:24 TLB).

A disgruntled, clock-watching Christian often brings a reproach on the name of Jesus Christ.

You may say, "Well, I don't like my job, boss, or supervisor." Without a doubt, you can give a catalog of justifiable reasons.

Joseph was innocent, falsely accused, and imprisoned. Did he become grumpy and rebellious? "In fact, the jailer soon handed over the entire prison administration to Joseph, so that all the other prisoners were responsible to him. The chief jailer had no more worries after that, for Joseph took care of everything, and the Lord was with him so that everything ran smoothly and well" (Gen. 39:22, 23 TLB).

Because of Joseph's good attitude and faithfulness, God was able to take him, the young slave prisoner, and make him the chief economist of Egypt; in fact, Pharaoh recognized the wisdom of God in the young man and said they had no one like him. And we today also cannot get along without the wisdom of God in our lives. When God promotes you, your company will also feel they cannot get along without you.

Do not steal your employer's time with the excuse that you

are busy doing something for the Lord. God will not bless stolen money nor will He bless stolen time.

Saul, the first king of Israel, was easily recognized in a crowd. He was a foot taller than everyone else. His physique and features were admirable and he undoubtedly was recognized as a born leader.

God had sent Saul to battle against the Amalekites and God blessed him in that battle. But Saul had decided not to destroy all the sheep, cattle, or all the goods. He thought he could appease God by giving Him a burnt offering. You remember the story I am sure. God is not interested in receiving an offering but rather obedience.

"Behold, to obey is better than sacrifice" (1 Sam. 15:22). And God, at that point, rejected Saul as king of Israel.

The importance of obedience to God and His Word cannot be overemphasized. Obedience to God's Word runs all through the Bible. Obedience will bring more joy and prosperity than all the sacrifices and so-called Christian service you and all your friends can amass.

IS IT GOD'S WILL FOR ME TO QUIT MY JOB AND LOOK FOR ANOTHER ONE?

This may be a difficult question to answer generally; however, there are some interesting tests or checks you can make by analyzing your answers to the following questions:

1. *Am I quitting because this job and the people I work with or for bug me?*

There was a laborer who once worked for me, whose attitudes would run the whole spectrum. One day he would be singing at the top of his voice or whistling. The next day he would be so angry he would throw whatever was at hand—a hammer, shovel, pick, or a timber. Generally, he would be fuming. One chilly morning he was directed to connect some underground plastic pipes to the downspouts on a new roller-skating rink we were completing. The exposed portion of the plastic pipes, not covered with soil, was exposed to the freezing night. Because of this cold temperature, the exposed plastic pipe became brittle and shattered rather easily. This brittleness, of course, made his job difficult. Caution and patience was needed when working with such pipe. When the exposed end was treated roughly it would shatter and require cutting and splicing.

I observed this workman. He was not singing or whistling this day but rather he was muttering to himself. On one occasion a piece of plastic pipe broke, making him furious. He turned to the building, which had exposed aggregate imbedded in the concrete walls, and cursing roughly, he took a swing at the wall with his bare fist. His knuckles began to bleed and hurt from the impact which made him even more furious. In his frustration he ran to his red pickup truck and sped out of the construction site onto the highway, almost hitting an oncoming car. I was later told he went down to a bar and devoured two straight bourbons, then raced to a nearby liquor store and bought two bottles and headed for his home. After walking into his bedroom, he reached into the dresser drawer and got a revolver, thinking he would commit suicide. First, he decided to call his brother and tell him good-bye, and as he was phoning, the alcohol in the bourbon took effect, giving time for his brother to call the police and minister. They all arrived at the home before he sobered up.

You may say you would not do that. It is likely you would not go that far, but do you ever get angry and fume? Talk to Jesus about it. It's probably that there is nothing really wrong with the job. Jesus can help you in any situation and under all circumstances.

2. *Have I completed the ministry God placed me in the job to accomplish?*

There can be no question about who gave you the job for "the steps of a good man are ordered by the Lord" (Ps. 37:23).

3. *Before you quit be sure you leave loving everyone.*

4. *Before you leave the job, first tell everyone about the good news of the saving love of Jesus.*

You may be the only messenger God will send to these people.

5. *If you are not doing the type of work you feel glorifies God, ask Him to provide you with one that does.*

6. *Will my quitting have a detrimental effect on my family who depend on the income from this job for their needs?*

7. *Will God get glory from my leaving?*

8. *Has God given me a better job to go to?*

Write out these questions with *honest* answers. Read them out loud before the Lord and God will answer you as to what you should do.

The unsung heroes will surprise many of the notables in Christendom when God rewards the people who had the small jobs in His kingdom, but were faithful. God's reward will be great.

Every pastor knows that his congregation is made up of individual members. A faithful member of the congregation is equally important in the kingdom of God as the pastor. If you feel your contribution to the kingdom of God does not amount to too much, think of Mary, the sister of Martha and Lazarus. The Bible notes that she sat and listened to Jesus and conversed with Him. Her faith was noted not in acts but in her willingness to listen.

If you feel second rate in God's plan, remember that God has no second-rate children. "God is no respecter of persons" (Acts 10:34). This means all 1700 scriptural promises are given to *you* as much as the biggest names in gospel show biz.

Sit at the feet of Jesus daily and converse with Him, and you will be choosing the most rewarding part. You will not be able to sit there long before God will use you for the important little things. He often cannot find anyone little enough in his own eyes to do such tasks because many feel they are too important for a small, unrecognized job. Jesus said Mary chose "the better part." This was more important than being the world's most privileged hostess. God is known for using people who are small in their own eyes.

Don't belittle the position God put you in but sit at the feet of Jesus and hear His voice—the greatest voice there is.

Abraham was a keeper of sheep, a vagabond in a strange

land. Even though he was a rich man, it is doubtful that others considered his life to be very dramatic. Yet, more people through the ages have called him father than anyone who ever lived.

Paul must have thought he was a failure, having to make tents to exist and spending a great portion of his Christian life in jail.

Perhaps some of you have had the opportunity to be in a managerial capacity and you've overheard someone say, "My job is too important for detail," or "I am not good at details." Right away you will know that this is a person you cannot put in charge of a department. It is generally no problem to assign the important jobs because everyone wants them, but in order to get the little projects done, which if not done when needed may stop the progress of the whole plant, the supervisor often has to do them himself. Can God use you as a supervisor to do the little things in His kingdom which seem to be too small for the people who are important in their own eyes?

Thank God for the job He has given to you. "The steps of a good [righteous] man are ordered by the Lord" (Ps. 37:23). The word "ordered" means directed. You may ask, "Is my low-paying job directed by God? It seems so unimportant. Why did He not make me a president of some big corporation or insurance company with an income of $100,000 annually?" Jesus said that if you are faithful in the little things He will make you ruler over many. Have you thanked Him for the little job He gave you and glorified Him in it? If you have, you can expect a promotion. When an important man does a dishonest deed, the whole world seems to hear about it. Would you want your actions, conversations, and attitudes to be broadcast to the whole world?

When you begin to praise the wonderful name of Jesus by your speech, actions, and attitude on your job, God will suddenly begin to work for you. There will be nothing man, Satan, or the world can do to hold the spiritual, physical, and financial blessings back if you practice this concept.

Joseph was rejected by his brothers as being worthless. He was sold as a slave to Potiphar in Egypt. He continued to praise God with his conversation, actions, and faith. In prison he was not afraid or ashamed to allow the gift of the Spirit of God to work through him in spite of the circumstances. Can you picture him day in and day out, which turned out to be years in and years out, praising God for His goodness without yielding to Satan and his suggestions? Notice God's power. One day he was a prisoner and the next day he was the ruler of the most powerful nation in existence. This was all done by the power of God, almost overnight. The greatest power in existence is with the Christians. That is why we are beginning to see so many of the leading business and professional men become Christians. When God can trust them with power He gives them power. Could you be trusted with $100,000 a year? Would you still have time to drive out of your way to pick up poor old sister Smith who has no way to Sunday school and help her from the car to the church door and back?

God has blessed many people with millions who are still going and preaching in prisons, the skid row missions, and weeping with sinners as they find salvation. They are millionaires made so by God but their money does not rule them; *they rule their money.* If you cannot rule the money you have, it is only the mercy God has for you that He has kept you poor so you would not be lost to the kingdom of God. When you become rich in your own eyes it is nearly impossible to get into the kingdom of God, but if God makes you rich, your riches can be to the glory of God with a joy and peace that is not sold at Macy's, K-Mart, or on 5th Avenue, but given to the children of God.

I was invited to speak to a group of businessmen at a luncheon in Oakland, California, and for some unknown reason I continued to expound on the Scripture about how Jesus said that His yoke was easy (Matt. 11:30). I suggested to the audience that if their religion was difficult for them, they had the wrong kind. At the end of the meeting a man about fifty-five years of age came forward for prayer. The following day this same man phoned and asked me if he could come to see me. At my invitation, he came and told me how he had been in a church all his life. In fact, he had attended a seminary for a period of time during his twenties. He never found the yoke of Christ to be light. We began to review the position of the people who accepted Christ but somehow were not totally yielded to the Spirit of God, like the Samaritans of the New Testament who were discussed in Acts 8. He expressed his desire to receive the Spirit of God. We had a short prayer and agreed to meet in another Christian businessman's home that evening where a prayer meeting was scheduled. This was an unusual prayer group held in the home of a Catholic food broker. The prayer meeting host described experiences and miracles similar to those ocurring in the early church. We arrived at the house after some searching; I was surprised to see the porch light was not on. In fact, we knocked on the door as if nothing unusual was really happening. However, after entering, we found about fifteen people of all ages. There were about three or four teen-agers, some middle-aged folks, both men and women, and even some in their sixties. Most were casually dressed and some were even sitting on the floor, in an informal atmosphere. My friend and I felt conspicuous, being the only ones in business suits, with ties and vests.

Those in attendance were very friendly and invited us in. In fact, they even embraced us. As the meeting began, they sang a couple of choruses and even forgot to open the meeting in prayer. They announced that the topic they were studying that evening came from Genesis. It centered around creation, one of the oldest subjects known—a subject discussed from grammar school through university classes. This topic disturbed me somewhat as I had brought a friend who was hurting and wanted a profound truth.

It soon became apparent that these people were unlearned in the Scriptures but their excitement was astonishing. They were finding out what was created on the first day of the week, the second day of the week and so on. My friend became increasingly nervous as the group continued talking about something neither of us had expected. The discussion continued for about an hour and one-half. Finally they announced they would pray for anyone with needs in their lives. The host assured us that God would answer their prayers that night, because God promised to give them anything they asked for. They were so simple and convincing.

My friend volunteered that he was a candidate for more of

God so the group gathered around my friend and said to him: "If you raise your hands we will pray and lay our hands on you and God will send the Holy Spirit into you." When his hands were raised, they all began to pray out loud. It sounded like a Chinese classroom. Then they all began to lay hands on him—some on his forehead and some on his shoulder and back. Then suddenly something happened. My friend fell to the floor as if he had fainted. At this point they all left him and began to pray for others; however, none of the others fell on the floor the same way my friend did. Soon I heard my friend praying but I could not understand what he was saying. After about twenty minutes he opened his eyes and said, "Let's get out of here!" So we excused ourselves and left.

When we got into the car, he began to tell me he had had a great experience with God and how God had filled him with His Holy Spirit and how he now knew that Jesus had taken the load of sin from his heart and had given him the joy and new birth in the Spirit. I have seen this man many times since and he continues to praise God for this experience, the same experience Christ talked to Nicodemus about.

What is so profound is that God so honored the house—this salesman's house—where people from all denominations came and received the very thing from God they had wanted for many years. Was it their teaching? Did it have organization or a certain format? What could it be?

In searching the Scriptures I find that only one of the disciples was a doctor. Most of the others were from more common walks of life. It was Peter, an unlearned fisherman, who preached with the power of the Holy Spirit on the day of Pentecost. In spite of his lack of training, 4,000 were converted that day.

Why such astonishing results? Perhaps God does it all if we just let Him do it instead of telling Him how to do it. "God hath chosen the foolish things of the world to confound the wise" (1 Cor. 1:27). Let God do it in your life. You will find Him the source of all good things.

11

RETIREMENT AND ESTATE PLANNING

Ninety-eight out of every one hundred people in the United States reach the age of sixty-five financially ill-prepared. Twenty-three out of one hundred *must* continue to work, seventy-five are dependent on others, and two are financially independent.

A network television station in San Francisco recently carried a series of programs depicting the extreme poverty of many elderly people in that city. They are poor in spite of the fact that most of them routinely receive Social Security payments and have Medicare benefits.

Many people I talk to have the misconception that Social

Security will take care of their needs once they reach retirement age. The truth is that these benefits will provide only a fraction of what is really needed. One day I was talking with one of the local Social Security interviewing officers. He stated that the intent of the Social Security program is to provide only supplementary income. It was never planned to be something one could retire and live on.

How sad, that only 2 percent of the people who reach retirement age are really prepared. They have lived over sixty years with little or no preparation.

Go to the ant, thou sluggard; consider her ways, and be wise: Which having no guide, overseer, or ruler, Provideth her meat in the summer, and gathereth her food in the harvest. So shall thy poverty come as one that travelleth, and thy want as an armed man. (Prov. 6:6-8, 11)

God's Word teaches us to plan for the future. God's plan for your retirement should start with paying your tithes, which carries a promise of blessing, and by saving and investing a portion of your current income. The government assumes you will provide most of your retirement support from these investments. It is amazing how even the Social Security system will not count dividends which you receive as a source of income from investments—whether it be from rents, interest, or annuities. You will receive full Social Security regardless of other investment-produced income. In fact, the government encourages you to save and invest.

I have found that a good rule of thumb is that one should

be actively preparing for retirement at least thirty years before retirement age. It amazes me how even a small amount regularly saved and properly invested will grow. For example, twenty dollars invested each week at 8 percent will grow to $127,240 in thirty years, a tidy sum to retire with. This sum will produce $848.26 a month in interest income perpetually without decreasing the principal. A nice supplemental addition to the Social Security payment.

Steady plodding brings prosperity, hasty speculation brings poverty. (Prov. 21:5 TLB)

Interestingly, this savings plan we are talking about is so simple and generally involves amounts much smaller than the average family frequently pays in interest charges on their credit card or time payment purchases. By proper planning you can literally "have your cake and eat it too." Putting a systematic savings program to work requires discipline in most phases of our lives. Let me illustrate: if you continued to eat all the food your stomach could hold, you would soon become sick. Similarly, if you continue to spend to the limit of your credit you will soon be financially sick and suffer both now and in your retirement age.

Not long ago someone asked me, "Why should I save for my retirement age? Jesus may come and then who will benefit from my savings?" I was not surprised at this man's question, for he had so overspent his income that his poor wife was frantic with worry that the mortgage company might foreclose on their house. His philosophy had been to spend his earnings and not to save. Now his wife and family are suffering anguish. This feeling of insecurity also causes the spiritual life in this home to suffer.

My answer was, "You should save for your retirement so that your family might not suffer now. Our heavenly Father provides for His children, so in like fashion we earthly fathers should provide for our families." I explained that when a person learns how to save, he, of necessity, takes a systematically organized approach toward his finances. The one who has not learned to save generally does not understand his spending limits and always has financial difficulties.

Estate planning. There are several qualified sources of help in this area, such as fianancial institutions, the trust department of banks, and religious organizations which can help you establish retirement objectives and suggest ways of meeting them. You need an expert in the field of tax consequence and ever-changing estate laws.

Many religious organizations, such as the Full Gospel Business Men's Fellowship, will be glad to help, generally without charge. Often larger churches will also have someone on the staff qualified to assist in estate planning. There is a difference between a Christian's will and a non-Christian's will.

Blessed is the man that walketh not in the counsel of the ungodly, nor standeth in the way of sinners, nor sitteth in the seat of the scornful. (Ps. 1:1)

You should use a Christian adviser whenever possible. What will happen to your assets when you die and who will get them are important matters. You may say, "I do not want to think about dying." However, by turning your head, death will not go away. I have attended funerals of Christians who had lived full lives for the Lord and for their families. Their funerals were celebrations of their glorious transformation from this earth to the heavenly realm. Naturally, their presence was replaced with fond memories, but in our hearts we knew they had passed from this life into the presence of Jesus.

The Bible states that one with a long life will live three score and ten years which is seventy years. So will I wait until I am sixty-nine to begin estate planning? Remember, many never come near that age.

Boast not thyself of tomorrow; for thou knowest not what a day may bring forth. (Prov. 27:1)

Estate planning is not limited to property and money. It should begin as soon as your first child is conceived. The Christian parent should name a Christian guardian for his child. Such a guardian will take over parental responsibility in the event something unforeseen happens.

You should also consider who will get your assets. Will your children benefit by inheriting your assets? Would you like to leave a portion to a good Christian cause? These are all questions that should be considered and planned for *now.*

You need a will, appointing a guardian over your minor children to continue their Christian upbringing. How tragic it would be after spending so much concern, time, and prayer that the selection of their future homes and families could be left to a court-appointed executor. There are many cases involving large families where the children have been separated from each other. I am sure those placed in executor positions seek to do their best, but they simply cannot think as you think, have the same priorities you have nor can they assume that one's children will be placed in loving, nurturing Christian families. The point is that this responsibility cannot be done by anyone but you. If you do not have a Christian will for your children, pray about it today.

Write your testimony in your will. It will be read publicly by people who may not know Jesus. Preach even when you no longer are alive.

We are enclosing a sample testimony that could be incorporated in your will.

LAST WILL AND TESTAMENT

I, __John Doe__, of the Country of United States of America, State of __California__, County of __Alameda__, City of __Livermore__, realizing the uncertainty of this life, possess full confidence and trust in my Lord and Savior, Jesus Christ, who said,

I am the resurrection, and the life: he that believeth in me, though he were dead, yet shall he live: And whosoever liveth and believeth in me shall never die. (John 11:25, 26)

I believe that He died for my sins on the cross and shed His blood as an atonement for my sins. I know that through my faith in His sacrifice on the cross, I have eternal life and admonish my heirs as follows:

But thou shalt remember the Lord thy God: for it is he that giveth thee power to get wealth. (Deut. 8:18)

And that my heirs remember that everything they have is in trust from Him and that they are only stewards of what He has given them, and pray that they will be good stewards. Being of a sound mind, memory, and understanding I do make and publish and declare this as my last Will and Testament, hereby revoking and making void any and all Wills by me at any time heretofore made.

Giving to propagate the gospel: If God has blessed you beyond your needs, give to the propagation of the gospel and help the needy. God pays good dividends. Seek counsel of others; it will help you to avoid pitfalls.

Where no counsel is, the people fall: but in the multitude of counsellors there is safety. (Prov. 11:14)

Why do you need a will?
1. It can provide a guardian for your minor children.
2. It can provide the most economical distribution of your property and estate with a minimum of delay.
3. It can conserve a maximum of your estate by minimizing taxes and other expenses of settling your estate.
4. It will enable you to give whatever portion of assets you stipulate to be used for the Lord's work.
Most Christians will agree that they should make a will, but in fact, only one out of eight sits down to do so. This indicates

some strong negative thinking which needs to be cleared up. Many think the making of a will is the last task one performs on this earth.

What happens if you die intestate (without a will)? The courts will distribute your property according to the laws of the state. Your relatives will share your estate, but probably not in the ratios or proportions you wish to specify. For example: If you leave a widow but no children, she may have to share your estate with your parents, brothers, sisters, nephews or nieces, in whatever way the law has decreed.

If you have children, your wife will probably be appointed guardian of any property you leave to your children. Most likely she will have to furnish a bond and pay bond premiums unless you make other provisions.

She would have to file an account each year, showing what she did with the children's share and she would have to go to court and explain the accounting.

Suffering and heartbreak can result through neglect to make a will. Recently a couple asked me the following question: "Do we need a lawyer to write up a will?"

My answer was, "Yes, making a will should not be a do-it-yourself undertaking."

Generally, any Christian estate planner will give you help in acquainting you with proper approaches you may take.

Then generally they will direct you to a lawyer who is skilled in estate planning and tax laws, whether federal or state. This attorney can custom make your will to suit your needs and accomplish what you want it to do.

For example: A widow with no relatives had an estate of $60,000. She made a will, leaving $10,000 to each of three charities and the balance to her church. At the time of her death, her estate had depreciated to $30,000 and her church received nothing. An attorney who understood her wishes could have stated that 50 percent of her estate would be distributed equally to the three charities and 50 percent to her church, thus her wishes would be properly carried out.

Blessed peace of mind and a sense of security accompany the knowledge that you have completed your stewardship to the best interest of your loved ones and to the glory of God and Jesus Christ.

"Moreover it is required in stewards, that a man be found faithful" (1 Cor. 4:2).

GLOSSARY OF TERMS USED IN A WILL

ADMINISTRATOR. A person appointed by the court to settle the estate.

BEQUEST. A gift of personal property.

CODICIL. A separate document making a change in the will.

CONSERVATOR. A court-appointed guardian of property or persons.

DEVISE. Gift of real estate through a will.

DOWER. The part of a husband's property inherited by his widow.

EXECUTOR. A man appointed to settle an estate.

EXECUTRIX. A woman appointed to settle an estate.

GUARDIAN. A person named in the will to care for minor children.

HOLOGRAPHIC. Hand-written.

INTESTATE. A person who dies and leaves no will or the condition of having died and left no will.

LAST WILL AND TESTAMENT. The legal document known as one's will.

LEGACY. Property left by will.

PROBATE. Proving the validity of a will and executing its terms under court direction.

TESTATOR. A man who makes the will.

TESTATRIX. A woman who makes the will.

TRUST. A right of real or personal property held by one party for the benefit of the other.

TRUSTEE. A person appointed to execute the trust.

BE SET FREE

Freedom is something every creature desires. One day I was asked this question, "Why do many Christians continue to experience unhappiness in so many areas of their lives?" I shared with them my forty years of bondage, attempting to live a Christian life during the entire period. It could be compared to the life of a pet my son Jerry had. This pet's name was "Barney" for he was a large barn owl. He had two big, brown eyes in the midst of white feathers on his face so arranged that they looked like two big, white mushrooms which had been turned upside down. Barney was required to continually live in a cage except for short periods of time when he was taken out for exercise. Even then, one of his legs would be fastened to a long chain.

When spring arrived, Barney began to screech, attracting other owls who could fly in freedom, and he could see them. Often they would return his call.

One night while Jerry was preparing to feed Barney, he neglected to close the door properly and suddenly Barney flew out and landed in a tree nearby. Jerry called and called, offering him strips of fresh meat, but Barney was free and refused to go back into the cage.

For more than forty years I was a faithful church member. Still, somehow, I felt as if I were in a cage and deprived of enjoying life. My learning began with catechism and continued through Bible school. I believed in the existence of Jesus and did the various things expected of Christians. In fact, I served as a deacon, Sunday school teacher, men's leader, and a faithful tither. Our family attended church regularly which is evidenced by my many plaques and awards for faithfulness.

In spite of all these activities, I continued to only endure my Christianity. It was almost like being in a cage, while being fed a man-made spiritual diet which at best did not taste good.

I remember a short period of time as a teen-ager when I had spiritual freedom. We had attended a prayer meeting where I experienced a closeness with God and was told that it was the baptism in the Holy Spirit. I remember I suddenly felt so clean and I hated no one and, in fact, I loved everyone. There was a lightness in my soul without any guilt or condemnation. This wonderful peace did not last very long because I again tried to fulfill what was called practical Christianity and its responsibilities. The numerous do's and don'ts soon frustrated me and before I realized it, the feeling of bondage and frustration returned.

When I attended Bible college many of my classmates seemed to enjoy freedom but it was not working for me. Life seemed so complicated. All other religious groups seemed to be in error except my own; in fact, we were required to write essays on their problems. I was anxious to do the right things, but my views became increasingly narrow. Instead of my religion giving me freedom, it became a bondage. I am sure it was the lack of total surrender. It may sound like a paradox but it is interesting to note that a surrender to God is not an act we do—it is yielding so that God can do the act in us. He takes out the old heart and gives us a new one.

God was so good to me to allow my health to so deteriorate that I considered my life almost finished. At that point I fully gave to Him the little that was left. To my amazement He not only healed me, but also set me spiritually free.

And thou shalt love the Lord thy God with all thy heart, and with all thy soul, and with all thy mind; and with all thy strength. (Mark 12:30)

Paul was told that it was hard for him to kick against the goads. In like manner, it is hard to live a Christian life without a total surrender to God. I am not only talking of salvation and confession of sins. I am talking of being yielded and putting ourselves in the hands of God for Him to use as He will. Are you willing to trust God for wisdom that you need spiritually, physically, and financially? God only permits disciples who are totally surrendered to Him. All your spiritual experiences occur with ease in God's presence and they bring joy and happiness. "But the fruit of the Spirit is love, joy, peace . . ." (Gal. 5:22).

Since I have escaped from the cage of bondage I am so in love with Jesus that I do not know the difference between a Catholic, Methodist, Pentecostal, or Baptist because they are all my brothers in Christ. No one could get me back in that cage again.

Do I continue to attend church? Yes, even more than I did before. In fact, each Thursday morning at six o'clock I attend a prayer meeting at the Episcopal church where a group of clergy and laymen from Roman Catholic, Assemblies of God, Methodist, Presbyterian, and Pentecostal churches check their doctrines at the door. With a binding, godly love, we worship, sing, clap our hands, and believe God for His will.

Every Saturday morning at eleven o'clock, I co-host a gospel radio broadcast from San Francisco with a charismatic Catholic salesman. We share the reality of Christ to a potential listening audience of several million people.

Sunday morning I attend Calvary Temple, and teach a Sunday school class.

Monday I attend a meeting of the Full Gospel Business Men's organization and Wednesday a Christian men's luncheon at a café in Livermore. In these meetings men find the Lord and experience a spiritual release. In addition to these many meetings, God gives me plenty of time to manage our ever-growing industrial park with two hundred tenants. This is not all. During the day I also counsel people about their spiritual and financial needs in my office. This is all done without frustration.

You may say, "My, all of this must tire you." On the contrary, I have never felt more alive than right now. My body has been healed and my spirit renewed. I always ask

Jesus how He wants these things done, and I never worry about the outcome, for that is His problem. My life is His and He is responsible for the outcome of every situation.

He has adopted me as His son, and He is always responsible for His children. It may interest you to know what has happened to me financially. God has blessed me each year since my spiritual release with more than I used to make in five years prior to my freedom in Him. You may say, "This does not make sense!" It is not supposed to.

But the natural man receiveth not the things of the Spirit of God: for they are foolishness unto him: neither can he know them, because they are spiritually discerned. (1 Cor. 2:14)

The wisdom of this world is foolishness with God. (1 Cor. 3:19)

If the Son [Jesus] therefore shall make you free, ye shall be free indeed. (John 8:36)

You may ask the question, "Why do you emphasize spiritual freedom in a book dealing with finances? Is it not God's responsibility to supply the spiritual needs, and ours alone to supply the physical and financial needs?"

The problem arises from following what is known as "half truths." One of these half truths often quoted is: "God helps those who help themselves." Although there is a truth in the statement, it is a half truth and is often even quoted by the thief or embezzler as a justification for his acts.

When the Bible states that the lazy will have poverty, it

does not suggest that we should try to work without God's guidance and help. When one loses the consciousness of God in the work-a-day world, frustration begins to set in and this leads to insecurity, the foundation for financial, spiritual, and social failure.

Come unto me, all ye that labour and are heavy laden, and I will give you rest. (Matt. 11:28)

When you recognize God as the guiding force in your life, your financial prosperity will *boom*. Attempting it yourself may keep you broke or *busted*.

It is amazing how eager God is to bless His children who obey and depend on Him for direction and guidance in every aspect of their lives. This happens to all who are willing to consider God's laws, whether they be physical, spiritual, or financial.

Train up a child in the way he should go: and when he is old, he will not depart from it. The rich ruleth over the poor, and the borrower is a servant to the lender. (Prov. 22:6, 7)

The Lord shall open unto thee his good treasure, the heavens to give the rain unto thy land in his season, and to bless all the work of thine hand: and thou shalt lend unto many nations, and thou shalt not borrow. And the Lord shall make thee the head and not the tail; and thou shall be above only, and thou shalt not be beneath; *if that thou hearken unto the commandments of the Lord thy God*, which I command thee this day, to observe *and* to do them. (Deut. 28: 12, 13 italics mine)

And thou say in thine heart, My power and the might of mine hand hath gotten me this wealth. But thou shalt remember the Lord thy God: for it is he that giveth thee power to get wealth. (Deut. 8:17, 18)

REFERENCES CONCERNING
BIBLICAL PRINCIPLES

Prosperity:
Gen. 39:3; Deut. 29:9; Josh. 1:6-8; 2 Chron. 26:5; 2 Chron. 31:21; Ps. 1:1-3; Ps. 35:27; Prov. 10:22; Prov. 28:13; Jer. 17:8-10; Luke 6:38; John 10:10; 2 Cor. 8:9; Phil. 4:19; 3 John 2.

Tithing and Giving:
Deut. 14:23; Prov. 3:9, 10; Mal. 3:10; Matt. 23:23; 1 Cor. 16:1, 2; 2 Cor. 8:13, 14; 2 Cor. 9:6, 8; Heb. 7:1, 2.

Provision of God:
Gen. 41; Exod. 15 (Moses).
1 Kings 17; 2 Kings 4 (Elijah).
John 21:2-6 (Peter).
Matt. 4:11 (Jesus).
Luke 12:7 (His People).

Wealth:
Deut. 8; Ps. 50:10-12; Eccles. 2:26; Luke 12:16-21.

Waste:
Gen. 41:36; Luke 15:13; John 6:12.

Saving:
Prov. 21:5, 20; Prov. 30:24, 25.

Prudence:
Ps. 112:5; Prov. 8:12; Prov. 12:16, 17; Prov. 13:16; Prov.

14:8, 15, 18; Prov. 15:5; Prov. 16:21; Prov. 18:15; Prov. 22:3; Prov. 27:12; Hosea 14:9; Amos 5:13.

Irresponsibilities:
Prov. 18:9; Prov. 24:30, 31; Eccles. 10:18; 2 Thess. 3:11; Heb. 6:12.

Investments:
Prov. 24:27; Matt. 6:19-21; Matt. 24:15; Matt. 25:14-30; 2 Tim. 2:4; 2 Pet. 3:10.

Inheritance:
Prov. 13:22; Prov. 17:2; Prov. 20:21; Eccles. 2:18, 19; Ezek. 14:16-18; Luke 5:11-31.

Debts:
Deut. 15:6; 2 Kings 4:1; Ps. 37:21; Prov. 1:17, 18; Prov. 3:27, 28; Prov. 22:7; Rom. 13:8.

Unjust Gain versus Honesty:
Deut. 25:5; Prov. 11:1; Prov. 16:8; Prov. 22:16; Prov. 28:8; Jer. 22:13; Luke 16:10; Rom. 12:17.

Budgeting and Planning:
Prov. 22:3; Prov. 24:3, 4; Prov. 27:12; Luke 12:16-21; Luke 14:28-30; Luke 16:1-8; 1 Cor. 16:1-8.

Accounting:
Matt. 18:23; Matt. 25:14; Rom. 14:12.

Attitudes:
Lev. 19:12; Ps. 112:5; Prov. 10:4; Prov. 13:4; Prov. 24:10; Eccles. 5:12; Mal. 3:5; Luke 6:35; Rom. 12:11; Eph. 4:28.

Discipline:
Matt. 7:13, 14; Luke 9:51; 2 Cor. 8:11; Heb. 12:11.

Facts about Finances and Personal Possessions:
Prov. 14:8, 15; Prov. 18:13; Prov. 19:2; Prov. 23:23; Prov. 27:23, 24; Luke 14:31, 32; James 1:5.

CONCLUSION

The walk of a Christian is exciting and fulfilling. When Jesus becomes our brother He takes our load, and we only walk alongside.

"Come unto me, all ye that labour and are heavy-laden, and I will give you rest. Take my yoke upon you, and learn of me; for I am meek and lowly in heart; and ye shall find rest unto your souls. For my yoke is easy, and my burden is light" (Matt. 11:28-30).

If you are laboring under great difficulties—financially, physically, or spiritually—review your fellowship with Jesus and your dependence on Him.

The Bible is like a company manual which lists all the parts to make your life function—spiritually, physically, and financially—producing total fulfillment.